Putting The User First:

30 Strategies For Transforming Library Services

by Courtney Greene McDonald

Association of College and Research Libraries
A division of the American Library Association
Chicago, 2014

The paper used in this publication meets the minimum requirements of American National Standard for Information Sciences-Permanence of Paper for Printed Library Materials, ANSI Z39.48-1992. ∞

Library of Congress Cataloging-in-Publication Data

McDonald, Courtney Greene.
 Putting the user first : 30 strategies for transforming library services / Courtney Greene McDonald.
    pages cm.
 Includes bibliographical references and index.
 ISBN 978-0-8389-8732-2 (pbk. : alk. paper) 1. Public services (Libraries) 2. Academic libraries. I. Title.
 Z711.M395 2014
 025.5--dc23
                    2014026445

Printed in the United States of America.

18 17 16 15 14   5 4 3 2 1

Table of Contents

Introduction

Just one simple idea can transform your library: put the user first. But as you likely already know, just because something's simple doesn't mean it's easy. From the website to the signage by the elevators—and even how our meetings are run—everything contributes to the overall user experience of our patrons. Yes, everything.

We want to do the best thing for our users but sometimes we don't, or we can't, or we try something we thought was best and we turn out to have misunderstood. Things change. It's a moving target.

User experience is everywhere. It's reference, it's your website, it's every phone call, it's the kind of experiences patrons have with your hourly student staff, it's your collections and it is definitely how many comfortable chairs you have and making the most of that prime window seating.

Some of us have buildings without windows (or without soft seating), many of us have shrinking budgets, nearly everybody has had grumpy colleagues and some days we—each and every one of us—are the grumpy colleague. The good news is that even small changes can make big headway. This book will give you thirty ideas for transforming your library and your services to be more responsive, effective, and user-centered through hands-on strategies and practical suggestions you can apply today. Some of the strategies might even transform you! I know they've changed me.

A warning about this book: user experience (UX) is serious business. Ultimately UX is what makes or breaks our success. This book, however, isn't particularly serious, if by serious you mean academic and neutral in tone, narrated in the third person, and dispassionate. The best user experiences deeply impact both the agent of delivery and the customer; they are highly individualized, very specific to a place or situation, and (we hope) enjoyable. This book adopts the same philosophy. You and I are going on a UX journey together in which I will share my experiences and insights and you'll contribute yours and hopefully in the end, we'll both say, "Hey, that was fun!" I would love to hear from you about where your UX journey takes you—please feel free to drop me a line at **users1st@gmail.com**.

USER GUIDE

Each entry introduces an idea or a strategy you can apply in your own practice or within your organization, frequently augmented by one of several follow-up activities through which you can choose to pursue the idea further. These include:

Actualize—Putting It Into Practice Yep, actually doing something.

Contemplate—Questions to Ask Yourself A time to put your thinking cap on and mull over some ideas or questions.

Investigate—Read More We are, after all, academic librarians so a reading list is never amiss.

To make this volume as useful as possible, I've notated certain characteristics of the various strategies within the table of contents, on each entry, and in a handy index. Here's a key to symbols you'll see used throughout the volume.

🕐	**No Cost:** That's right. These won't hit anyone's pocketbook directly—they will cost you only time and effort.
💲	**Low Cost:** These can be accomplished with a very modest investment.
⚙	**Technological:** Strategies that can be applied to web and tech things; but don't worry, most don't require heavy-duty tech know-how.

	Physical Spaces: Contrary to popular belief, UX is not only for the web. Apply anywhere in your library.
	Personal Practice: These you can do all by yourself; just integrate into your own thinking & practice.
	Organizational Culture: Here's where you can take your colleagues along with you.

#1   Admit

This first step is a big one—everything else in this book hinges on this one idea. If you can take this in, understand it, believe it, internalize it, make it the first thing you think of every time you even contemplate doing anything public-facing in your library, you will have laid the groundwork for success in putting your user first. Here it is.

You are not your user.

Yes, you use your library too. That doesn't count. Yes, you have amassed valuable personal experiences and observations of user behaviors that help you understand. Still doesn't count. *You are not your user.* Understand this: you can never go back to being a civilian again. You, who understand the mysteries and power of controlled vocabulary, the arcane magic of proxied access to electronic resources—you can never go back to the time when you might have innocently typed a series of random words in a box and hit search in a demonstration of utter and unthinking trust in the power of the search engine to deliver the "right" or "best" results. You, who can effortlessly interpret the meaning of words and phrases like monograph, festschrift, and summary holdings statement, who routinely triumph over partial (and even patently incorrect) citations with specialized weaponry like the *Encyclopedia of Abbreviations* and the *National Union Catalog Pre-1956 Imprints*—you could never again stand on the sidelines and say something like, "I just need a source for my paper. Any of that stuff would be fine."

Those days are over for you—and that's something to celebrate, because you have a deep and nuanced understanding of the structure of information in a variety of contexts, as well as expertise in the often complicated and sometimes confusing systems that make access to that information possible. On the other hand, though, this has two important effects on how you navigate through a library environment, whether physical or digital:

1. You notice more things (and different things) than a non-librarian user, even an expert one. Proof: upon viewing a search results page cluttered with data, a librarian will instantly zero in on subject descriptor terms like *Manhole covers in art*[1] or *Boxing—Corrupt practices—New Jersey.*[2]
2. You ignore more things (and different things) than a non-librarian user, even an expert one. A librarian will say, almost instantly upon scanning a results set, something like, "Oh no, not that one, it's only a review; and not that one either, it's from a questionable press."

Thus we come back to the crucial idea: *You are not your user.* So forget thinking that you are. In most other parts of life, we are indistinguishable from the population we serve, passing freely among them. It can seem like nothing is different. But, to borrow from the parlance of a well-known and influential organization: the first step is to **admit** that you have a problem—in this case: *you are not your user*, just in case you forgot. Take heart, though, because this "problem" is also the very thing that makes it possible for you to engineer solutions: you are on the inside and you can make changes to the way your users encounter the library. Why, here you are reading this book looking for tips on improving the user experience at your library. You are already on your way to making the twisting, turning paths of research straight and plain for your constituents … or maybe even just making it easier to figure out where the bathrooms are through better signage. These are each noble quests.

Be advised that this shift in thinking is going to take a constant re-education process on your part. By the way, this maxim is true for every UX professional everywhere, not just librarians, so there's loads of UX literature on this topic.

---

1. http://lccn.loc.gov/sh2012003287
2. See http://authorities.loc.gov/ (It doesn't have a permalinked authority record but I promise it's there.)

INVESTIGATE

Before you feel discouraged—or maybe you just want to get even more pumped up about this UX journey—check out the writing below.

Gócza, Zoltán, and Zoltán Kollin. 2014. "Myth #14: You Are like Your Users." *UX Myths*. Accessed April 18. http://uxmyths.com/post/715988395/myth-you-are-like-your-users. This site, UX Myths, is a must-see.

Hess, Whitney. 2012. "The User Is Not Like Me." *Pleasure and Pain*. http://whitneyhess.com/blog/2012/05/04/the-user-is-not-like-me/.

Porter, Joshua, and Joshua Brewer. 2010. "You Are Not Your User." *52 Weeks of UX*. http://52weeksofux.com/post/385981879/you-are-not-your-user.

Spool, Jared. 2010. "Actually, You Might Be Your User." *User Interface Engineering*. http://www.uie.com/articles/self_design/.

#2 Define

Now that we have definitively established that *you are not your user...* who is?

Knowing your users—the ones that are uniquely yours to serve—is key to developing a great user experience. I'd like to pause and say here, "This task was appointed to you, and if you do not find a way, no one will."[3] But that would be really, really nerdy, and also not quite true; as we've seen, there are numerous parties ready and willing to serve our patrons, including but not limited to Google, Amazon, and the neighborhood outpost of a large book chain.

Returning to the question at hand (to recap: not *where is the ring?*[4] but *who are my users?*) I have observed a tendency to jump to one of two extremes in answering it:

⇒ Broad strokes.
Example: *We support the teaching and research goals of our students, faculty and staff.* Granted, this is completely appropriate for a mission statement, but it will be very hard to evaluate honestly and effectively. This really doesn't give you a manageable research question to take out into the field and measure. You could actually stop now and say, "We've succeeded!" At this level of definition, you certainly have.

⇒ Minute specificity.
Example: *Professor Plum brings her intro to philosophy classes in every semester to do that scavenger hunt she developed in 1985 so we've built a mini-site to support them with a list of all the 72 books she uses.*

---

3. Jackson, *The Lord of the Rings*.
4. Ibid.

I am not against supporting assignments (in this case, I don't think it would be going too far to call it 'serving as angels of mercy for these unsuspecting undergraduates') but expanded across the entirety of either your web site or your in-person services, this approach is going to result in, at best, a patchwork quilt and at worst, a sort of volunteer fire brigade constantly rushing to address the most recent crisis.

How then, does one **define** the unique community served by your library or institution? Some might say it's strictly quantitative: pull the numbers collected by folks in your Admissions department and look at metrics you collect in the library—your population is 28% underrepresented minorities, 41% undergraduates, 15% non-traditional college students over the age of 25, of whom approximately a third are heavy library users. Others might counter and say it's a deeply qualitative exercise, that a user population is as varied as the unique users of whom its comprised, and that we experience this best through focusing on becoming acquainted with them and with their stories. My response to this is: why feel you have to choose? They'd both be right.

Our user communities are always changing, and an accurate picture is arrived at slowly, incrementally, through a process of mashing up your broad strokes and your minute specificity with a heavy dose of structured, purposeful observation. And because, in academic institutions, our population turns over with some regularity—not to mention the world in which we all live is constantly changing—this information will shift over time. So you get to do this forever!

As in most research, though, you are going to begin with a hypothesis that will need to be tested and refined through data collection. In the next portion of the book we'll outline some strategies to help with this part, but for now, start by focusing on the questions below. Once you've taken some time to think through them, boldly set pen to paper (or fingers to keyboard) and see what you come up with as a first overall definition of your user group.

CONTEMPLATE

⇒ *Your elevator speech*
How would you describe your institution (focusing on its people and their interests) during a short elevator ride to the following people:
- o   A library administrator from another institution?
- o   A former colleague you haven't seen in several years, with whom you were quite chummy?
- o   Your favorite celebrity, who's somehow indicated to you that s/he *might* be willing to throw some money at your library if you can sell it right?

⇒ Mulling over your experience at your current library, who are your repeat customers? What elements of your campus community do you rarely or never see inside the library doors?

⇒ Think of a couple of statements or measures frequently bandied about by your institutional admissions department ("dynamic young faculty," "wonderfully diverse," "academically rigorous, attracting the best and brightest under-graduates"). Note down where you see evidence of that in your day-to-day experience working with patrons. Now think of two examples (just two for now! and keep them positive) of daily encounters with user groups who don't fit into those pictures, and briefly outline their characteristics.

#3   Observe

"Carlyle said that how to observe was to look, but I say that it is rather to see, and the more you look the less you will observe ... what I need is not to look at all, but a true sauntering of the eye."
—Henry David Thoreau[5]

Much of the time in our work environment, we're highly focused on a particular task, goal or outcome—arriving to that meeting, heading to a desk shift, getting that coffee in hand—so even if you already make a point of spending time in the public spaces of your library building, or other in other highly trafficked spots across campus, you may or may not have been at liberty to really observe what was happening there.

We have some thoughts about our user population and certainly we have some ideas about what they are doing in our spaces or elsewhere on campus, but have we really taken the time to experience that recently? (You'll notice I didn't say to *document*—I said to experience.)

Each of our buildings, however small or large, serves many different functions. For each of the spaces in your building(s), there are patterns to be noted for anyone who takes the time to **observe** them. Who do you see? What are people doing? What are they talking about? Are they alone? Do they come in groups? Do they use it as a hangout, a safe space for meeting, a hiding place, a place to focus and get work done, a passthrough on the way to somewhere else, a dry place to wait for the bus? Are they working with your furniture or against it? What are the staff focused on? For spaces with technology, who's using it and how—academically, recreationally, both, neither? How does this change over the course of the day, the week, the semester or academic year? How are all these answers different as you move around? Later, you might ask yourself how the patterns you begin to tease

---

5. Thoreau, *Journal*, IV: May 1, 1852–February 27, 1853:351.

out within a library space or spaces differ from those you might notice during time spent in the student center or other places on campus.

One thing about patterns though—some of them might jump out at you right away, but to be sure you are seeing what you think you are seeing you'll need to watch them over time. Thoreau's "true sauntering of the eye" tends to be something we busy creatures of the 21st century, with our constantly chirping devices and our easily diverted attention, need to take some time to relax and ease into.

Essentially, you are lurking, a concept we understand from social media—you're there, observing, but you're not actively participating yourself. In real life, it's important to be careful to toe the line and not to accidentally tip your lurking over into creepy—at which point you would be skulking instead of lurking. Is your student newspaper a huge hub of information exchange on campus? How do they report on events, on places, on the library? Start reading the paper and it won't take long to find out. What sorts of advertisements or marketing campaigns really strike a chord on your campus? A couple of years ago at Indiana University Bloomington the campus started doing a series of PSA type announcements with plastic "party animals"—including a giraffe "spokesperson."[6] It's totally taken off ... proof that sometimes you can never guess what will work.

ACTUALIZE

What I'm going to suggest may be difficult, even though it's quite simple, because in many ways it runs contrary to our notions of productivity, it flies in the face of pressing deadlines and urgent e-mails, and it chokes on a busy schedule.

---

6. Indiana University, "Street Smart."

Go somewhere in your library, dressed like someone who doesn't work there (no nametags!), park yourself for an hour or so, and soak it in. Take a notepad, an iPad, a laptop or even a book to help you blend in, and later, to give you a place to make notes of questions that arise in your mind, or notable and unexpected uses of space or items.

Most people are so busy with their own pursuits they'll stop noticing you pretty quickly. If you work in a very tight-knit community, flying under the radar may prove more difficult at first but persistence will soon make you part of the scenery. In my experience, undergraduates in particular are marvelously un-self-conscious about "old" people [that is, anyone over 22] and will say interesting things. Traffic flow tells its own tales. Move on to other spaces in your building and other places on campus.

Get into the social media spaces that are big in your community—or get into them all to see what *is* big in your community—and observe. How do people behave in these spaces? How is it different than what goes on in another similar space? Are there noticeable norms specific to your community in each particular platform? See what's happening. Finding out what they are saying about your library, or that they aren't yet saying anything about your library, is only one of the benefits. More than ever people are posting their feelings, their expectations, their reactions to the places and brands they experience in their day-to-day. What does it all mean for your organization?

You can take things a step further and begin to monitor commentary about your library by setting up a series of searches in a Twitter client such as Tweetdeck[7] or Hootsuite.[8] The first, and easiest thing to do, is to set up a search for the name of your library. You could also set up a search with geolocation information and target all tweets within a certain range of your location with particular terms in them.

---

7. Twitter, TweetDeck.
8. HootSuite Media, HootSuite.

Oh, and one more thing: don't begin your experiment on a library account. Pause and do a bit of learning on your own. Create your own account, follow or connect with your own personal community and with organizations you'd like to observe or emulate. Get a feeling for the ebb and flow of the channel first, then feel free to begin building out your library's presence in the space.

#4   Notice

> *"The trick to finding ideas is to convince yourself that everyone and everything has a story to tell. I say trick but I mean challenge, because it's a very hard thing to do. Our instinct as humans, after all, is to assume that most things are not interesting. We flip through the channels on the television and reject ten before we settle on one … We filter and rank and judge. We have to. There's just so much out there."*
> —Malcolm Gladwell, *What the Dog Saw*[9]

Figure 1: Yin & Yang, Tiger Girl (Flickr)

---

9. Gladwell, *What the Dog Saw and Other Adventures*, xiii.

If you think of the previous strategy as the yin of experiential observation, this strategy is the yang—a more active noticing.

What color is the house or building next door to where you live? What about the one three doors down? What is the first thing your guests see when they enter your house from the front door—or from the back door? How many water fountains do you pass once you've entered the lobby of your building before you get to your office? At your place of work, how many parking spots for the use of visitors with disabled parking permits are there, how far are they from the door, and where is the next closest group of them? How many clicks does it take to access your full staff profile on your library's website? No, I can't rattle off the answers to all of these either (although I can answer the first one—white). Some of the answers don't really matter very much, and some answers matter a lot.

When things are shiny and new, they're fun. People on vacation take photos of all sorts of things they'd ignore at home. When you walk into a building for the very first time for a job interview, it's easy to pay attention to all of its good (and bad) points. As time goes on, this slows and then stops. We tend to get used to things. We ride the same bus to work everyday and hardly look up from our books. We walk in our buildings and don't really see the furniture or the signage or maybe even broken machines. We explain the six step process to accomplish a basic task, either because we've gotten used to it, or we've given up that it will ever get better, or maybe both. We are, perhaps, a little surprised that people don't know that the thus-and-such collection is on the shelves furthest from the windows in the room at the end of the hall on the north side of the first floor. We step around the accumulated boxes in the break room. We roll our eyes at that one colleague who *always* asks a million questions or who *never* seems to "get it."

This is human nature. Everyone does this somewhere. Remember the last time someone was a little bored, maybe a little rude, when you asked a question at that store you'd just visited for the first time? Uh-huh. How about that one restaurant you don't like to go to anymore because everything is so crowded—or the chairs are really uncomfortable—or they make you do a silly song-and-dance about reservations? Yep. Or when the person closest to you finished your sentence for you, a trifle exasperated ... except that wasn't what you were going to say? Exactly.

Some of our users—the ones who are in our space every day, perhaps—might be, like us, a bit insulated in their experiences about our space, a little bit inured. Most of them aren't. They **notice**. It's pretty important that we make a point of seeing what they're seeing and that we are alive to what they are experiencing.

CONTEMPLATE

Try to mentally revisit your space, your library—even your own attitude—with fresh eyes. What would it look like if you'd never visited before? How would you describe you if you'd just met you? Wow, that one's kind of meta. But I think you get the idea. Where are things working? Where might you be able to do a little cleanup—rearrange, do a little light dusting, offload some unnecessary items, delete a page or two? Are there places crying out for a full-scale overhaul?

#5   Serve

I am not talking about servant leadership (although I think that, too, is a good idea). I am talking about public services, service desks, reference, information desks, concierge, Ask A Librarian, telephone reference, IM reference, text reference, orientation fairs—whatever. Quickly, before some of you flip to the next page, I'd like to ask two questions:

⇒ Are you interested in knowing what interests your user community? The sorts of things people out there are doing with your website? What makes people spontaneously say, "Hey this is awesome!!!"?

⇒ Would it be helpful to know where users are running into roadblocks of jargon, of difficult workflows, of policy, of missing features? Put plainly, would you like to know where you are currently missing it?

I chose those questions because I firmly believe that if you didn't answer a resounding YES to both of them, you might want to take a few moments and seriously contemplate whether user experience work is for you. User experience is about being curious, it's about fixing things, it's about continuous improvement, but it is only about all of those things as they relate directly to people.[10]

Where can you simultaneously do all those things? At a public service desk. Can you work on a public service desk? Then do. Do you work on a public service desk? Drain every drop of use out of it. Let me say, so you don't write me and complain I didn't warn you: every

---

10.   It is very, very hard and unpleasant to be a passionate, empowered and fulfilled UX professional (and, I would venture to add, librarian) if you don't like interacting with people—and it's not a lot of fun for the people around you either. I'd go so far as to say it's no way to spend your life. You can be curious, fix things, and continuously improve in lots of other settings and quite likely be much, much happier doing so. I hate to think of people unhappy and trapped in their jobs. Mull it over. Be free!

shift is not going to be packed with revelation and a-ha moments—but they will be there, and on the days when it's slow you can catch up with your e-mail or build more rapport with your colleagues or do a little mentoring of your student employees or maybe just even smile at the four people who walk by and ask you nothing. Some people feel that working at an information desk, answering a lot of 'where is' and copier and restroom questions is a waste of their time or possibly somehow beneath them. If the concept of servant-leadership comes into this discussion at all, it is now. It is at this point that I would like to reference the title of this book—*Putting the User First*, and inquire sincerely: have you ever asked directions—of anyone? needed change, or to know where you could park? Was that information helpful to you? Did it, occasionally, change your day for the better?

Trying to explain your processes over the phone, the palpable desperation of the person who cannot see the sign for the restrooms, attempting to type out in an IM window how you do "X," looking someone in the face who is near tears over her paper and realizing that it may have been partly due to bad planning but the distress is real and right at that moment your catalog is not making things easier for her, being fervently thanked for looking up a title or providing a tissue or chasing down an incredibly obscure footnote or fixing the stapler—you are now living the user experience, my friend. This is where it gets real.

Being busy is no excuse. If you can only do one two-hour shift a week, you will learn something. Other than being expressly forbidden from doing so by your supervisor, the only acceptable reason for not working at a public service desk, not agitating with your reference department and supervisor to allow you to be trained and **serve** in this capacity, is: you come to realize you don't really like interacting with people. Then, definitely don't do it, and please consider reading the footnote on this section.

INVESTIGATE

These are a few of my favorite things. While my husband calls himself a technologist with a library problem, I myself am nothing if not a reference librarian so nerdy I wound up in a job mostly about technology. I hope that's something I share with you, dear reader, but if not, I think you'll get something out of these resources anyway.

Lang, Walter. 1957. *Desk Set*. Running time: 1 h 43 min.
Lankes, R. David. 2011. *The Atlas of New Librarianship*. Cambridge, Mass.; [Chicago]: MIT Press; Association of College & Research Libraries.
Taylor, Robert Saxton. 1968. "Question-negotiation and Information Seeking in Libraries." *College & Research Libraries* 29 (March 2): 178–194.

#6   Obsess

We've all probably seen the quote (on the Internet), "The real voyage of discovery consists not in seeking new landscapes but in having new eyes," attributed (on the Internet) to Marcel Proust[11]; apparently (according to the Internet[12]) he never said that exactly at all.

Whoever said it, however it was said: once you start thinking about user experience, you too will look at things (even and possibly *especially* on the Internet) with new eyes. There's not going to be an activity for this strategy because you are probably already doing it, and it is: notice UX stuff all the time, everywhere you go.

People may begin to tell you that you are a nut. They may ask you to stop ranting about the terrible user interface of the ATM; they will probably roll their eyes while you exclaim about how poorly the application installed on the cash register of that place you went for lunch met the needs of the wait staff (not that you will notice). As you are shopping for shoes (on the Internet) you will note with delight the effective faceting displayed in the sidebar and as you wrestle with self-assembly furniture you will scowl with disapproval at the poor instructions. If you really take to this you will even begin to armchair quarterback customer service interactions, wondering how *you* would have chosen to handle the tricky situation with the bad policy and the worse behavior from the customer in question as you wait in the queue at the home improvement store.

In this one way, it's OK to **obsess** a little. Become a bloodhound for the scent of anything you sniff out that rings a bell in your mind of, "wow that was easy"—or, conversely, crashes the gong of "get me outta here."

---

11. Proust, "The Real Voyage of Discovery... at BrainyQuote."
12. Yahoo! Answers, "Where Does This Quote Come From?"

Why? Well, it's good practice, for one. It'll put you in a mode of meta-thinking about your day-to-day life and that will trickle over into your work and you'll get all sorts of brainstorms about how to fix things. (N.B.: If you wind up rearranging your entire kitchen or reorganizing all your closets or adopting a new and improved way to mow the lawn, you go ahead and take the credit with your impressed family and leave me out of it.)

The other edge this will give you is flexibility in your thinking. There's a great story (on the Internet) about Kleenex®. It started out as one thing[13]—maybe or maybe not the lining of gas masks for World War I, although that's on the Internet[14] too—and wound up as a cold cream remover, which was a big hit in the 1920s. Obviously its uses have transitioned with the times, although for loyal users of cold cream I'm sure it still works just as well. You never know what the next great UX breakthrough for libraries is going to be, and the more you focus and activate your thinking, the more likely it is to be you who thinks of it. When you do, though, whatever it is, be sure to put it on the Internet. I want to read about it.

---

13. Kimberly-Clark Worldwide, Inc., "The Kleenex® Brand Story."
14. "Kleenex."

#7   Sift

We all get a little dirt thrown on us sometimes, in the form of patron complaints, a dart or two lobbed by coworkers, or maybe snarky comments from higher-ups; we witness some mule-like opposition to change, a vigorous spate of foot-dragging, or may even be so lucky as to receive a flat-out cease-and-desist order. Sometimes it's as simple as someone not agreeing with you, and telling you so a little louder, a little more intensely or a little more often than you'd like to hear. Into every life a little rain must fall, as they say. But if I may be permitted to say (and I am, because this is my book), you need both rain and dirt for flowers.

Now, you aren't going to be able to do a lot with some of the insightful commentary from the free-text box of a web survey along the lines of "your liberry sux!!!!!!!!!!!!!!!!!!!!!!!!!!!!!!!!!"—it will suffice to add a hashmark to the 'complaints' column. But, in nearly every other criticism or dissenting opinion, however obnoxious or crazy it may seem, there is a germ of truth. Well, maybe not *every* one: I heard tell of someone comparing a change to a library web site to the burning of the library at Baghdad (... um, wow). But you get the idea.

As I've travelled along in my career, I have come increasingly to value negative, critical, questioning or dissenting feedback. I vigorously **sift** to see what remains when the outer husk of the method of delivery, the source, even my attitude or emotional reaction, has been peeled away and discarded. It helps me see things from a different perspective. It frequently shows me an area in which my expertise is limited. It often reveals a blind spot. It certainly highlights a pain point. It can show you a break down—this is a great way to get insight into 'cracks' where your users are left stranded between places, or thwarted from making the connections. It can often uncover or reveal causal relationships between systems that you might not have connected without that feedback loop.

In user experience work, this is what we want to know most, correct? We like to know where things are working well, but we *need* to know where things are broken and the pointy bits are stabbing people. As the leader or advocate for a project or service, we also need to know where we have failed to effectively communicate the vision, and sometimes that's what a complaint reveals. Occasionally a complaint can reveal that it is the complainer him- or herself that might be a bit broken, but I find this to be a fairly rare case. And when it is, I try to take that opportunity to be part of the solution. [see **#23 Smile**].

Remember: though we mightn't have solicited these gripes, problems, complaints, screeds, disagreements, criticisms, or bug reports, they are feedback and feedback is valuable. Take hold of the opportunity to do something with the weighty things that are left after you've sifted. (see **#17 Listen**)

INVESTIGATE

This isn't exactly fun stuff, but once you begin to get a handle on it, it's very powerful. I found that these books help break down the process in a way that gives you a place to start.

Fisher, Roger, William Ury, and Bruce Patton. 2011. *Getting to Yes: Negotiating Agreement without Giving in*. New York: Penguin.
Stone, Douglas, and Sheila Heen. 2014. *Thanks for the Feedback: The Science and Art of Receiving Feedback Well (Even When It Is off Base, Unfair, Poorly Delivered, And, Frankly, You're Not in the Mood)*. New York: Viking.

#8   Ask $⚙◪

Patron-driven acquisition. User-centered services. Participatory design. These are all wonderful, inspiring ideas and it is amazing how quickly they can drop right out of notice and roll away on the floor when a new, shiny gadget or trend or buzzword bursts in the front door. It happens to the best of us (and even to me!).

It's easy to talk a big game about user experience design and careful crafting and suchlike and yet somehow find yourself planning and building and launching things without pausing to check in with anyone in the target audience. We all get carried away sometimes. Instead, start by conducting a needs assessment. It's true, needs assessment sounds kind of serious and involved and like it might require a lot of paperwork and basically just be nothing but a huge delay, because after all, the new thing is happening right now! And we don't want to miss the boat! And yes, it can be all of those things, but is there *any* process that a determined group of people can't make serious, involved, paperwork-heavy and slow? Experience suggests no.

A needs assessment can be conducted just as nimbly as you like, if you put your mind to it, and it is an invaluable early-stage step in nearly any project. I was going to say "in every project" but I think we can agree that a needs assessment might not be necessary all the time—before putting up a new display or replacing those computers from 2001 or even telling that one department they can start a blog and see how it goes, for example. It is simply this:
1) asking real people real questions
2) right where you are
3) about what they are doing and thinking and planning
4) with a focus on some particular service or tool or idea you are mulling over
5) then writing up what you discover

6)   into a recommendation
7)   with an initial plan.

Or I could put it this way: "… the impetus to create new services shouldn't just come from a hunch or a hope; a needs assessment is integral to planning. By undertaking a needs assessment in some form, you'll have a better understanding of how to serve your users in this area. You'll also have something concrete to refer to in discussions with administrators and staff."[15]

You can develop a short survey, set up at the entrance to your library, and see who stops. You can plan focus groups with multiple segments of your population. You can feed some people pizza and talk with them about what they think. You can contact colleagues at peer institutions and ask what they've done and how it's working. You could finish each IM reference interaction with a single question on a topic. You can crunch some data (see **#11, Evaluate**). The point is: there are lots of ways to **ask**, and the best way to do so will depend on what need you're assessing. As we say to our patrons: just ask.

I must end this section with a caveat: If you're going to ask for ideas and changes then you'd better be prepared to do something with them. This doesn't mean you can't do something different than what was suggested; and it doesn't mean that you are obligated to do something with every piece of input. Think of it this way: once you've asked about a particular topic, service, or idea, your audience responds, and then it's your turn to make a move. It's actually better not to ask at all than to ask people for their thoughts and then take no action on the matter, so consider this when you are about to solicit feedback.

---

15. Greene, Roser, and Ruane, *The Anywhere Library: A Primer for the Mobile Web*, 4. Yes, that's our other book, and no, I couldn't come up with any better wording than Missy's for that idea this time either.

INVESTIGATE

There are as many ways to do needs assessment as there are needs or libraries. Here are some resources that offer a variety of examples.

Dudden, Rosalind F. 2007. *Using Benchmarking, Needs Assessment, Quality Improvement, Outcome Measurement, and Library Standards: A How-to-Do-It Manual with CD-ROM*. New York: Neal-Schuman Publishers.

Greene, Courtney, Missy Roser, and Elizabeth Ruane. 2010. "It's Never Too Late…But Can It Be Too Early?" In *The Anywhere Library: a Primer for the Mobile Web*, 2–8. Chicago: Association of College and Research Libraries.

Royse, David D. 2009. *Needs Assessment*. New York: Oxford University Press.

WebJunction. 2012. "Needs Assessment." http://www.webjunction.org/explore-topics/needs-assessment.html.

Witkin, Belle Ruth. 1995. *Planning and Conducting Needs Assessments: A Practical Guide*. Thousand Oaks CA: Sage Publications.

#9   Curate

I'd like to advocate for the importance of curating content: not in a way of keeping people out, but in the sense of

- presenting someone a beautifully wrapped package of things that hold together
- sifting out the chaff for them so they can make sense of your search results
- polishing and paring so it's easy to accomplish important tasks
- highlighting a few special things you'd like to share

Think awesome book display. A website that's great for mobile and desktop users. Clear signage. When you take the time to **curate** your content, you put the power in the hands of the user—if they want more, let them take the next step.

A beautifully wrapped package of things doesn't just assemble itself from a bunch of copy written at different times by over a hundred voices. It doesn't magically coalesce (with a wink from a magical fairy) when your web committee gets together to discuss priority links for site-wide navigation and ends up stuck on fonts. Book displays don't shimmer into reality overnight. Signage is usually everyone's problem, and (alas) nobody's sole responsibility.

My colleague Anne Haines recently gave a lightning talk at Confab Central, and I'd like to pull a sparkling gem of truth from her abstract: "In an academic research library, 'KEEP ALL OF THE THINGS' is a legitimate part of our mission. While that's a useful mission when it comes to books, it spells disaster for a website."[16]

Curation requires intentionality. Intentionality requires a strategy. A strategy requires ownership.

---

16. Haines, "New on the Work Blog."

Enter content strategy. What does that mean? "Content strategy is the practice of planning for the creation, delivery and governance of useful, usable content."[17] There are a lot of important concepts in there, but right now I'd like to focus on two: planning and governance. Having a plan for our content goes beyond saying, "Let's make a laundry list of our services and resources and write about all of those." It means thinking about what needs to be said to whom, why, where, in what context, who's going to write it and—very importantly—who's going to keep checking back to see that everything remains up-to-date, and relevant.

This brings us to the second big idea: governance. While we're pretty comfortable with the part of governance that revolves around measuring usage data, it seems like we run into trouble at a couple of stages:

a) the part where we do something with that usage data, like cut pages that aren't used; or even

b) the part where we agree who's in charge of the content and thus entitled to make such decisions.

When armed with sufficient data to back up the decision, a style guide, and an articulated content strategy, the content owner should have the ability to prune content. If you don't, I'd venture to hypothesize that you might not actually own much of anything, except the headaches. We talk a lot about our interfaces and workflows, but—"If you take content strategy out of the mix, you marginalize one of the key components of a successful user experience: the content."[18]

Further, without content ownership being the specific purview of a person or department, undertaking crucial but admittedly difficult tasks like a content audit is going to be slow, probably not very organized, and possibly not very effective. A content audit is just what it sounds like: an inventory of what's there, how old it is, what it's for, and who created it. In addition to ensuring that you can plan adequately (pretty important if you are going to

---

17. Halvorson and Rach, *Content Strategy for the Web*, 32.
18. Ibid., 167.

be strategic) a content audit will help you identify ROT. In content strategy terms, ROT stands for stands for "redundant, outdated, trivial."[19]

If that's not inspiring enough—Erin Kissane points out that even James Bond relies on his team to provide him with timely, appropriate content: "Content is *perfectly* appropriate for users when it makes them feel like geniuses on critically important missions, offering them precisely what they need, exactly when they need it, and in just the right form."[20]

So, when it comes to curating your content, make sure you have a solid content strategy, then Live and Let Die.[21]

INVESTIGATE

These three volumes are authored by the acknowledged leaders in web content strategy—they're the tops, and they've changed how my department and I think about our work.

Halvorson, Kristina, and Melissa Rach. 2012. *Content Strategy for the Web*. Berkeley, CA: New Riders.
Kissane, Erin. 2011. *The Elements of Content Strategy*. New York: A Book Apart.
McGrane, Karen. 2012. *Content Strategy for Mobile*. New York: A Book Apart.
U.S. Department of Health and Human Services. 2014. "Content Strategy Basics." Usability.gov. April 21. http://www.usability.gov/what-and-why/content-strategy.html. *A Great Quick Overview of the Essential Ideas, and a Good Supplemental Reading List.*

---

19. Allen, "ROT."
20. Kissane, *The Elements of Content Strategy*, 5.
21. Hamilton, *Live and Let Die*.

#10 Escape

"To get away from one's working environment is, in a sense, to get away from one's self; and this is often the chief advantage of travel and change."
– Charles Horton Cooley[22]

Librarians are really swell people. Libraries are pretty awesome too. I'm betting that for quite a lot of us, routinely, when you go on vacation you are inexorably drawn to the nearest library. Some of us might even *plan* trips around libraries we want to visit. It can be very inspiring to visit other libraries and see what they're doing and how they do it. Talking with other librarians can happen in lots of ways, around the water cooler or at conferences or brown-bag discussions or unconferences or meet-ups or tweet-ups or even just coffee with someone from across town. I have derived great professional benefit from the communities of practice that have sprung up inside or outside of formal meetings, and have been amazed and astounded at how they have grown in influence and impact through continuous interactions via Twitter (or other means) unfettered by geographic proximity.

That said: great athletes cross-train. Or that's what I read, anyway. For deeply unsporty types like myself, let me try again: a balanced diet includes all the basic food groups. Go see what others are doing. Talk to some non-librarians. Read UX literature that originates outside libraries. Read other stuff altogether. Variety is the spice of life, after all.

Now let's consider another angle: athletes schedule rest days so they don't overstrain, and even we champion eaters better take some time off from hitting it hard now and then. These days where technology fits into your pocket, the Internet is always on, and you can work "from anywhere" (um, yay?) it can be hard to keep in balance. Step away and let it all percolate from time to time, and you'll be much more productive than if you

---

22. Cooley, *Human Nature and the Social Order*, 219.

are always only one notification bleep or bloop away from the mothership. One more note: sure, burnout is no good for you and your personal relationships, but it's also hard on your colleagues. You're not going to be much of a poster child for UX librarianship in your institution if you're the resident grouch. Last but not least, it's hard to put the user first when you are at the end of your rope.

Obsessing about UX is great. Adopting a user-centered way of thinking, diversifying your reading, exploring other arenas—these are helpful and important. But call it quits sometimes and just **escape**, do something fun, go a whole day and don't mention libraries at all, be lazy and lie under a tree, leave your smartphone at home, bake bread from scratch, refuse to check your e-mail, use an ATM without criticizing the interface, spend quality time with people you love, make something 100% analog, get a pedicure, institute a one-day social media blackout, watch a game, whatever floats your boat. Just because we *can* doesn't mean we should, as my mom likes to say, and that goes for being 'on' and working all the time too.

For those of you struggling to justify this and those who reject it out of hand, there's actually a solid business reason for a little R&R. It turns out that innovation and serendipity hang around together—this pair has been known to perform as the "a-ha moment." As you feed your brain a more diverse diet of ideas by talking to other librarians and by taking in ideas from other fields, you give it something to work on. But, like a fire, it needs a little space and oxygen to really combust: "Serendipity ... develops initially from a foundation of action. However, the foci of activity is (sic) not the territory of the ultimate serendipitous discovery: it may be *some other field*, or it may be *just the process of activity itself*."[23] [emphasis mine]

In other words, it's turning your attention to other things that sets the tinder ablaze. That's when you are primed to have a really great insight into something you can do, something you can change, something you can stop doing that will really impact how your patrons

---

23. Martello, "Serendipity as an Entrepreneurial Tool," 81.

experience the library. (This technique is also effective when the something else is a different work project, which I cover in a later section, **#28 Play**.)

I don't know about you, but now I'm thinking I might just try and nap my way to greatness.

INVESTIGATE
More food for thought.

Coleman, Jackie, and John Coleman. 2012. "The Upside of Downtime." *HBR Blog Network*. http://blogs.hbr.org/cs/2012/12/the_upside_of_downtime.html.
Johnson, Steven. 2010. *Where Good Ideas Come From: The Natural History of Innovation*. New York: Riverhead Books.
Martello, William E. 1992. "Serendipity as an Entrepreneurial Tool." In *Academy of Management Best Papers Proceedings*, 80–84. Academy of Management.

#11 Evaluate

The great thing about user experience work is that there's something for everyone—intuitive, people-oriented, gut-decision, arty design types? Definitely. Super data-driven number-crunching statistics nerds? Absolutely. This tip goes out to the latter.

In libraries, we love data. Metadata, data sets, books about data, plain old data, data with whipped cream and a cherry on top ... so the first step will be to figure out what information you have at your disposal. What all can you look at? We have many services, service points, users, and use scenarios.

Do you have instant messaging transcripts? Gate counts? Hashmarks about reference transactions? Usage data from Google Analytics? Transaction logs from your catalog or website server? Information about space or computer usage? Database usage statistics? These, and the many other data points we might choose to review, are all to some degree tangled up with one another. So when reviewing information from so many sources, ask yourself: can any of them be reliably and sensibly cross-referenced?

Next, once you have a sense of what metrics are available to you, take some time and think carefully and deeply about what it is that you want to know. Serendipity can be very helpful in some situations but being adrift on a sea of data is both terrifying and a waste of time. The base questions are obvious: How is this service doing? Should we keep doing it? Should we let it go? Should we change it? Very rarely will these questions be easy to answer because there are simply too many factors and variables.

How do we navigate through the thicket of data? To avoid individual bias, always retain a firm grip on reality in the shape of a clearly articulated, measurable, and meaningful research question. This will enable you to enter into your Excel spreadsheets with a purpose, show SPSS who's boss, neutralize NVIVO—you get the picture.

Finally, remember this:

Stories + math =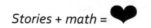

We've probably all heard the saying, "Statistics never lie but liars use statistics." Liars use words too, so I'm not proposing we stop using either statistics or words. Your numbers can't explain themselves and anyway, all the numbers we collect are really about people—what people are doing, what it seems like they can't or don't or won't do, maybe even a little bit about the how or why. This equation also ensures that you involve everyone in your findings, the intuitive, people-oriented, gut-decision, arty design types and the super data-driven number-crunching statistics nerds and everyone in between.

INVESTIGATE

Look, people, I was an English major; I can crunch data but it's not like everyday I'm walking around seeing zeros and ones superimposed on everything. Here I present you with some examples of analysis that have inspired me, plus a stats book that might prove useful for the beginner.

Hurst, Susan, Andy Revelle, and Aaron Shrimplin. 2013. "Seeing the Forest by Counting the Trees: Using a Variety of Data Sources to See the Big Picture." *Journal of Web Librarianship* 7 (4): 434–50. doi:10.1080/19322909.2013.835175.

LaGuardia, Cheryl. 2013. "My Friend Sarah, the Library Data Analyst." *Not Dead Yet [Library Journal]*. http://lj.libraryjournal.com/2013/04/opinion/not-dead-yet/my-friend-sarah-the-library-data-analyst-not-dead-yet/.

Salkind, Neil J. 2008. *Statistics for People Who (Think They) Hate Statistics*. 3rd ed. Los Angeles: Sage Publications. (Thanks to my colleague Andrew Asher for this suggestion.)

#12 Pretend

Yes, I remember what I said in **#1**. But this is about user personas.

What's a user persona? I was so hoping you would ask that. Let's start with what a user persona is not.

A user persona is **not**:
- A detailed description of your favorite patron.
- A detailed description of your *least* favorite patron.
- A thinly veiled description of yourself or anyone on your staff.
- A highly fictionalized account of your ideal patron.
- A real person. Not even a little bit, not even at all.

A user persona is:
- A fictionalized description of an iconic user;
- Representative of the typical behaviors and motivations of an entire user group;
- Based on collected data.

Why do you need them? Tell me if this sounds familiar at all.

> "Who's going to use your product?"
> "Everyone!"
> "And what will they do with it?"
> "Everything."[24]

---

24. Kuniavsky, *Observing the User Experience*, 129.

If your experience is similar to mine, you've heard that before. A website (or product or service) aimed at everyone generally succeeds in pleasing no one. What to do? User personas can help.

> ... User profiles allow you to focus on specific images of users that everyone on the team can reference and use as sounding boards for development ideas. They're also much simpler to work with than 'everyone.' ... [Using user personas] quickly gives you insight into what makes a good user experience and can keep your product out of the 'everything for everyone' trap.[25]

Typically user personas are named so as to create easy shorthand amongst the UX team:

> "Susie would totally want to use that citation index because she'd have heard it mentioned by her faculty advisor. How can we make it clear to her how it works?" ...

> "Are you kidding? Jorge would never cheat on JSTOR! That's his favorite." Etc?.

Sometimes this can lead to confusion, and after you've spent a bit of time working with a persona, calling them by name and thinking about what they'd like and what they'd do, you can start to feel like s/he is real. Do not plunge into the Pygmalion trap and fall in love with your own inanimate creation. A persona is a collection of facts and characteristics, sometimes laid out in a narrative format, to which you have assigned a handle for easy reference. You could name them things like K, or Blueberry, or even HAL9000. (I would strongly recommend against *Rebellious Computers* as a naming convention, however.)

In fact, just to further emphasize this idea that a user persona is a useful narrative construct and nothing more, I'd like you to pause for a moment and think of the film *The Matrix*.[26]

---

25. Ibid., 130.
26. Wachowski and Wachowski, *The Matrix*.

There were some real people—like Keanu and Carrie-Anne Moss and Laurence Fishburne and that one guy who almost always plays a whiny villain—but there were a lot of fake people that were really just bits and bytes, like the lady in the red dress. They weren't really there. Think of these named user personas more like that latter group—they only exist in your mind to help you project out to a larger group. User personas give us a productive, structured way to **pretend** in order to improve our interfaces and services. Just bear in mind: there is no spoon.

INVESTIGATE

If you have not already begun to map out the segments of your user population in a methodical, data-driven kind of way that will support meaningful research from a user experience perspective, there are some tools you can use to help you begin to think about this. What's listed below is just the tip of the iceberg.

Cooper, Alan. 1999. *The Inmates Are Running the Asylum*. Indianapolis, IN: Sams.

Kuniavsky, Mike. 2003. "User Profiles." In *Observing the User Experience: A Practitioner's Guide to User Research*, 129–157. San Francisco, CA: Morgan Kaufmann.

O'Conner, Rob. 2011. "Personas: The Foundation of a Great User Experience." *UX Magazine*, March 25. http://uxmag.com/articles/personas-the-foundation-of-a-great-user-experience.

Tempelman-Kluit, Nadaleen, and Alexa Pearce. 2012. "Persona Most Grata: Invoking the User From Data to Design" presented at the LITA National Forum, October 8, Columbus, OH. http://www.slideshare.net/nadaleen/persona-most-grata-invoking-the-user-from-data-to-design-14605604.

Unger, Russ. 2012. "Personas." In *A Project Guide to UX Design*, 2nd ed., 129–144. Berkeley, CA: New Riders.

#13 Prioritize

This is another one that is really simple, but not at all easy. In these days of shrinking bud-gets, fewer staff, and more demands, it is important that we come to terms with the fact that we cannot do it all, cannot fix it all, cannot be all things to all people. We never could, actually—but who knows. In some other times it might have been a tiny bit easier to think so. Also, since this book is at least marginally focused on the technological—trying to do, be, or fix it all is a really quick recipe for a terrible, terrible website. Avoid.

Here's how you can start to **prioritize**. Pick a population. Any population. Now keep that population in your mind ...

Artisanal cheese makers!

No?

The point is: Make a choice about what constitutes your primary population. Then identify one or two others as secondary populations. Finally, put the remaining groups in a tertiary set—no, they're not ignored, they're simply kept aside until called for.

This is the time that you go back to what you learned in **#2 Define** and use that informa-tion to evaluate what's on the table to be done, and how it fits in with your users, your mission, your areas of strength as an organization.

Setting priorities requires honest conversations, difficult admissions, thoughtful justifi-cations and hard choices. It requires patience. It requires collaboration, which is never to be confused with consensus. It will likely necessitate that you undertake what I've heard described as "disagree but commit." It will almost certainly mean that you stop doing things—historically a huge difficulty for us in libraries. (See **#14 Stop.**)

Putting things in order of importance can be unsettling because once you have decided what really matters, you have also decided what doesn't matter so very much, or perhaps even what things no longer matter at all.

Why is this admittedly uncomfortable process important? As it happens, I have a few ideas about that.

1) If you can't clearly and passionately articulate to your colleagues why something is important, how in heaven's name are you ever going to be able to do so in a larger arena with teaching faculty, Provosts, Trustee members, or the general public, most of whom seem to generally like libraries but few of whom understand what we do—and all of whom hear many competing calls for the few minutes (or simoleons) they have to dole out?

2) Most of your users will not lobby for themselves: they'll either find that you are providing what they need and thus keep coming back; or, they'll have one or more unsatisfying interactions with your library, conclude there's no value for them there, and quietly wander away. For every comment-card-writing, Dean-calling, desk-shouting edge-case there are hundreds more who just press the off button and move on. I don't say this to preach doom and gloom, and I know that there are many, many satisfied patrons out there with whom you have flourishing relationships.

Let's dream bigger and start a library revival! What do you say? I'd like to see whole campuses converted to where the library is a central part of daily practice, across the board, every day. Identifying your primary audience, then making their priorities your priorities is a fail-safe strategy for future-proofing your library, and it works like this: you take their stated need ("access to quality resources" "inviting study space" "data management expertise"), you run it through the lens of your professional library expertise and expectations, and you hand it back to them bigger and better than they could imagine. Often people know they need something but are unaware of the potential sophistication or scope of the available solutions, so let's wow them. Everybody wins.

CONTEMPLATE

So, why are you doing what you do, anyway? Could you, right now, tweet what your library priorities are? If so, bravo! But I suspect fewer of us are in that camp than you might think. If you don't know what your priorities are professionally—for yourself and your career, in terms of what librarianship means to you, for your institution—how are you going to advocate for them? Know thyself, Socrates.

It took transitioning to a position in an ARL[27] library for me to realize just what I am: a radically populist generalist with a huge soft spot for the undergraduate. A geeked-out reference librarian. A confirmed glass-half-full technoluddite Pollyanna. This might seem like a lot of self-indulgent piffle to you but it has really helped me sharpen my sense of where I am coming from in any given situation, what I might have to offer conversationally and professionally, and how my own biases might need to be taken into account. In so doing, I think it is making me a much more productive member of my community.

Try it. I dare you. Then tweet me your personal taglines (I'm @xocg, hashtag it #idareux).

---

27. The Association of Research Libraries is "a nonprofit membership organization comprising 125 research libraries in the US and Canada representing universities, public libraries, national libraries, and special libraries." (http://www.arl.org/)

#14 Stop

A long-winded section titled "Stop" seems like the height of irony, so I'm going to cut right to the chase.

- You can't be everything to everyone. What stuff can we let go that could better be done elsewhere?
- It's painful, but it must be said: retirement should not be the only socially acceptable reason to discontinue a service.
- No is a valid answer.

Sometimes we all get a bit too personally associated with our projects or spaces or ideas, which can lead to messiness and hurt feelings if those things end up at the bottom of someone's list, or are slated for discontinuation. Know when to say when. Sometimes the best thing to do is just ... **stop**.

Together we are better sounds really inspirational on a t-shirt or logo but it can really burn you when *together* we decide that *we* really don't want to invest in building that cool new citation system for your faculty and instead we *are* going to buy all new printers for document delivery because that will be *better*. It's great when your brainchild comes out on the top of the heap, but as they say: sometimes you get the bear, and sometimes the bear gets you. Sometimes the bear gets something that you thought you really should save for later on "just in case" but really it was just some stale odds-and-ends left in the chip bag, and one partly-consumed granola bar. Even if it was something truly yummy that you did want to nibble on later, do you really want to wrestle with a bear over it?

The big takeaways here:

1) Job #1 is to align with your organizational mission and goals.[28] It can be the awe-somest idea ever but if it doesn't fit at your place of work—then it's not awesome. Or, you might need a new place of work, but that is a decision between you and you and your budget and your personal judgment and I have nothing to say about *that*.
2) "Because we have been" or "we always have" are not acceptable justifications for doing anything.
3) Libraries are not the only game in town. To give kind of an over-the-top example: gmail is already gmail; people don't need a library gmail. Let the big spenders build some stuff and don't try and library-ize it by building it yourself. If you must library-ize, then do so through finding some way to add value to the existing service by helping people use, understand, or build upon whatever it is in the context of the pursuits through which you relate to them.

The end.

---

28. As stated in the ACRL Standards for Libraries in Higher Education: "Libraries must demonstrate their value and document their contributions to overall institutional effectiveness ... Local outcomes and metrics should be tailored to the institutional mission, goals, and assessment practices." (http://www.ala.org/acrl/standards/standardslibraries)

ACTUALIZE

Good habits begin at home, as they say. So the activity for this section is a personal one[29]—and yes, I have taken my own advice and done just what I am recommending to you, many, many times over. Whip out a pocket mirror, take a good, long, hard look at yourself and say:

- Self, what things are we doing every day at home that maybe should be questioned? Anything that can be downsized, weeded, discontinued? Are there places where we feel a bit pinched (for time, space, etc) where clearing a little space might be a breath of fresh air? Let's write those down.
- Good job, self. Now, what things are we doing as part of our practice at work that might fall into the same category? Hold on—we don't mean giving a good old slash-and-burn to our position description to get rid of the icky bits. This is more methods-based, the how in how we work. Any new leaves we might want to try turning over there? Ah, good. Make a note of those too.

Then, don't try and quit them all at once. Cold turkey is only good on sandwiches. Pick one from each pile and give it a go ... I mean a stop ... you know what I mean. See how that works out. After a bit, move to another. Next stop: so much more time and energy! (Do you see what I did just there? Yep.)

You may be amazed at how your renewed vigor inspires your colleagues ... and the stop revolution starts to go.

---

29. Tempting to start with a big laundry list of *All the Things At My Library That Need To Go*, I know, but please see **#25, Defuse**

#15 Connect

Libraries are special places. We collect all sorts of things: information, books, media (Realia! Ephemera!). We classify and sort them so they can be retrieved. Academic libraries do all of this in the context of higher education, an environment that rewards, encourages and relies on differentiation. A scholar's career in academia may begin with general education requirements, but as a lifelong pursuit, success depends upon cultivating expertise: delving deeply, thoroughly, to explore and amass understanding on a highly particular, well-defined area of inquiry within a discipline. Like so many nodes in a network, the faculty as a whole—a connected network of specialists—make possible the breadth and depth of learning which characterizes a university.

On a day-to-day level, from the perspective of us folks trying to serve our community, this can sometimes tend to focus attention on heterogeneity—how are these things different? Faculty are different than undergraduates in the following ways. Humanists prefer this method of presentation. Scientists will gravitate toward these sorts of sources.

Sure, there's value in appreciating the differentiations of needs and preferences within our user population (see **#13 Prioritize**) but I'm concerned we sometimes take this parsing too far. To my mind, before we get to the point where we can turn our focus primarily to differences in user preference or behavior, we really would need to feel that we had the basics down pat. I'll freely admit that's not something I can state with confidence. As a person who works on interfaces that serve lots and lots of people, my first set of goals revolves around attempting to make the basic connections happen smoothly, efficiently, transparently for everyone—finding an article, placing a hold on a book, locating the subject specialist, determining whether the building is open or closed.

I'm reminded of the Sesame Street song; there are a few versions, but one[30] goes,

> One of these things is not like the others
> Which one is different, do you know?
> Can you tell which thing is not like the others?
> I'll tell you if it is so.

I find that the longer I'm in this UX racket, the more I hone in on the similarities in the needs of my users rather where they're different—and there are a lot of similarities. If you can make a high-demand service like renewing books easy-peasy across the board, it'll work for your faculty and for your undergraduates. I celebrate and admire my colleagues who are subject and domain specialists but in so doing, let's not undervalue the skills of the generalist, whose job it is to think about everybody all the time and to focus on commonalities. We rely on subject and departmental liaisons to give us in-depth feedback on their communities, but as the user experience professional, our duty is to take all of those reports, review them, and **connect** the dots that will enable us to make large-scale improvements.

This focus on finding points of connection leads to better interfaces but it also leads to stronger collaborations—user experience work happens in a community. The way I see it, the UX person or department ought to be one of the most connected and connective people on the library staff—after all, our work intersects with everyone else's, impacts everyone else's, and at our best, it brings all the various strands of doing and thinking into one harmonious whole.

This starts with your working team, expands out into the circle of people you intersect with on a regular basis, and then expands to your what I think of as your "reach contingent"—those connections you have to work a bit to keep up. If possible, strive to include a range of people in your Reach Contingent, including but not limited to:

---

30. Sesame Street—"One of These Things..." (Bird Seed).

- On-campus colleagues in the library with whom your work rarely intersects. Faculty and staff from non-library departments. Extra points for non-library users with whom you can make non-library connections.
- Beyond campus within your library system or consortium, or libraries with whom your library most closely works on a regular basis
- People from institutions that are nothing like yours at all

While it is obviously helpful to talk to your counterparts, don't forget that there is also a lot of value in seeking out folks whose day to day responsibilities are focused on the areas you are most interested in expanding, or whose work is totally removed from yours. The more inputs you have, the more complete your information is and subsequently the better the potential quality of your end product.

💡 *CONTEMPLATE*

There's no time like the present to get started with this. Take a few minutes to think over who might be the charter members of your Reach Contingent.

- On-campus colleagues in the library with whom your work rarely intersects.
- On-campus faculty and staff from non-library departments.
- Beyond campus (within your library system or consortium, or libraries with whom your library most closely works on a regular basis).
- Librarians from peer institutions.
- People from institutions that are nothing like yours at all.
- Someone at a "Dream Team" institution.
- Someone you see as a mentor.
- Someone who sees you as a mentor.

#16 Care

It's easy to talk about the importance of connecting with your community, but walking the talk takes a lot of commitment. Making deeper connections requires us to care—to be invested, to put a stake in. Past a certain point, it's not cool to care; many of us spent a lot of energy in our teens (and even our early twenties) giving a command performance of languid boredom. But, let's review: we're librarians. We aren't doing this only to be cool, are we? I hope not. Why do we do this? Because we **care** about our patrons, about learning and teaching, about providing a great user experience—how we might choose to go about our day to day might be different, but I imagine a lot of the really big ideas that keep us going are the same.

In fact, focusing on *why* you do what you do is the best way to stay motivated. You might have heard of Simon Sinek's book, *Start With Why*, which discusses the idea that people and companies that really make a difference do so because all their actions outflow from the underlying idea or principle that motivates their work. In an ACRLog post, Steven Bell advocated developing a 'why' statement for our libraries that articulates why we do what we do. This kind of statement is "… about believing that our work is going to make a difference—but only if we pursue our cause with great passion. It is not merely a result of our activity. It is a reason to perform the activity."[31] Doing something in the service of a bigger, overarching why tends to lead to more satisfaction in one's work, too.

A few years ago, there was an excellent article in *The Atlantic* about a longitudinal study Harvard conducted of nearly 300 men, and its findings about what factors may or may not contribute to lasting success and happiness. Some of these might not be surprising: education, not smoking or abusing alcohol, some exercise, stable marriage, employing mature psychological 'adaptations' (responses to stress or distress). What's interesting

---

31. Bell, "The What Versus The Why."

is how George Vaillant, longtime director of the Grant Study, summed up the findings overall:

> In an interview in the March 2008 newsletter to the Grant Study subjects, Vaillant was asked, 'What have you learned from the Grant Study men?' Vaillant's response: 'That the only thing that matters in life are your relationships to other people.'[32]

So: Care. Care desperately. Care for the sweet patrons, for the problem patrons, for your grouchy colleagues, for the people that make you look forward to going into the office, for those freshmen who are talking loudly about beer in the library lobby. Dare to care.

Before we all grab hands and sing Kumbaya together, pause to consider what this means: relationships come at a cost. They're great, but they're messy.

> ... why, [Vaillant] asked, do people tell psychologists they'd cross the street to avoid someone who had given them a compliment the previous day?

> In fact, Vaillant went on, positive emotions make us more vulnerable than negative ones. One reason is that they're future-oriented. Fear and sadness have immediate payoffs—protecting us from attack or attracting resources at times of distress. Gratitude and joy, over time, will yield better health and deeper connections—but in the short term actually put us at risk. That's because, while negative emotions tend to be insulating, positive emotions expose us to the common elements of rejection and heartbreak.[33]

Caring is often inconvenient, and it nearly always requires us to step outside ourselves. As with anything that has the potential for great benefit, it carries with it a considerable

---

32. Shenk, "What Makes Us Happy?," 46.
33. Ibid., 48.

amount of built-in risk. Sometimes it's just plain awkward—or scary. My response to this: why not be optimistic, maybe even unwarrantedly optimistic? Making a lasting investment in people seems like about the best why I can come up with, frankly. As my grandmother says, there is always time to be disappointed later if things turn out badly, but if they don't, you won't have wasted your days being down in the dumps over something that worked out great. And, if you get burned a little bit, you can always employ one of those mature adaptations George Vaillant talks about and come out a bit more grown-up.

INVESTIGATE

I think developing a personal why statement might be a very profitable exercise—perhaps an outgrowth of your personal tag line from **#13 Prioritize**. Before doing so, some food for thought:

Bell, Steven. 2011. "The What Versus The Why." ACRLog. http://acrlog.org/2011/05/10/
the-what-versus-the-why/.
Shenk, Joshua Wolf. 2009. "What Makes Us Happy?" *Atlantic Monthly* 303 (5) (June):
36–53.
Sinek, Simon. 2009a. *Start with Why: How Great Leaders Inspire Everyone to Take Action*. New York: Portfolio.
———. 2009b. "Simon Sinek: How Great Leaders Inspire Action." Filmed Sept 2009.
TED video. 18:05. Posted May 2010. http://www.ted.com/talks/simon_sinek_
how_great_leaders_inspire_action.html.

#17 Listen

I hope nobody will tune me out on this one, because though it's simple, I have found it to be really important. This is another one of those things that we've all been hearing since kindergarten, and if we'd paid attention, well—I wouldn't need to write this section, for starters.

People tell us all the time about our services, our collections, our staff; they drop easy wins in our laps; they give us wide doors of opportunity to be strategic, innovative, successful. They have no idea they are doing all of this, and by and large we don't know they are either, sadly enough. As the people running the joint, we should be able to recognize patterns—either problem patterns or positive patterns—in the ongoing dialogues we have with our users and staff and then take advantage of that intel.

Listening is not the same as hearing, as we all know from having had someone repeat back to us, mindlessly, the last three words said; or, worse, having done that to someone else. You don't have to agree with someone to **listen** to her; you don't even have to empathize with him, although as a UX professional I find empathy helpful when it fortuitously descends (or when I can muster it up, see the previous section **#16 Care**). You only have to focus on engaging with what that person is saying—really hearing it and processing it—and responding to it. Sometimes you can respond in the moment, and other times perhaps you just thank that person for taking the time to comment and accurately note down their observations for later consideration.

There is always something to be learned from the expertise and experience of those around you. In fact, there is no better way to learn than through asking. In his excellent book *Humble Inquiry: The Gentle Art of Asking instead of Telling*, Edgar Schein advocates for the importance and power of asking questions:

It has always bothered me how even ordinary conversations tend to be defined by what we tell rather than by what we ask. Questions are taken for granted rather than given a starring role in the human drama. Yet all my teaching and consulting experience has taught me that what builds a relationship, what solves problems, what moves things forward is *asking the right questions*.[34]

Albert Einstein was quoted by Moszkowski in *Conversations with Einstein* as saying something similar: "Most teachers waste their time by asking questions that are intended to discover what a pupil does *not* know, whereas the true art of questioning has for its purpose to discover what the pupil knows or is capable of knowing."[35]

This can happen at work, too. Let's use our questions to build up, not break down. This is not the part where you attempt to convert this person to your point of view; that is not what UX work is about. Hopefully in doing your work you will convert people to your point of view—i.e. *you are not your user; focus on the experience of the person on the other end of these things we are building or doing; reduce complication, increase ease*—but as most people have experienced, nobody really likes someone telling them how to think, or which of their opinions or habits need changing.

Much of my current job involves foisting new and unfamiliar things on my colleagues (New website! Different interface! Changed process!). I've found I have to be intentional about remembering that not everyone enjoys this, and then consciously bringing encouragement, patience and empathy to my interactions. As technologists who are constantly confronted with new and unfamiliar things, you'd think we'd have more sympathy for other folks as they have those experiences but it can be all too easy to forget.

Fair warning: a lot of times when you start listening the folks to whom you are listening will bring you what seems to you like a whole lot of odd sized baggage and just drop it

---

34. Schein, *Humble Inquiry*, 3–4.
35. Moszkowski, *Conversations with Einstein*, 65.

there. [By the way, this is the only time it is acceptable to sift through someone's luggage and find the items of value (figuratively, of course).] Or, sometimes they'll begin by unpacking some dirty laundry—*You are doing this wrong. It should be different. This was hard. I hate it.* (We've covered that in **#7 Sift** already.)

Persistence in listening will be rewarded. Here we're interested in things like:

> That page was pretty ... where are the hours listed again? [Uh oh. Interface problem.]
> Oh! I didn't know I could renew online. [Uh oh. Probably another interface problem.]
> [*Any statement that one could translate as "I just took an unnecessarily circuitous path to get to something that was linked from the home page"*]. [Ditto above.]
> Where are the bathrooms, ad infinitum. [Signage problem.]
> *From staff:* We get a lot of questions about how to recall. [Interface problem, workflow problem, and possibly also a policy problem.]
> I don't make requests anymore. [Weep. Then Ditto above.]
> I call the public library first 'cause they're really nice and help me know how to ask better and then I call you and ... [What kind of problem is this not? Although props to the public library.]
> You lied about that service. [Again, what kind of problem is this not?]

So that's not hard, right? Two ears are pretty much standard issue. You just have to start really using them and your brain at the same time. And then prepare for the accolades to roll in.

ACTUALIZE

This should be easy. What three questions/complaints/requests for explanations do you hear most often? Is there anything you can do about those? Also, do some 'on the street' interviews with fellow staff who work at different public service desks—what are their top three? Is there anything you can do about *those*?

Find a librarian or two that are active instructors and ask each what local process or resource is the most complicated to teach. By now you should know what's next: Is there anything you can do about it that would make it less complicated?

Keep going until you have a list of a dozen or so. Solve, delegate, escalate. Rinse and repeat.

#18 Translate

When I was growing up our family business was a restaurant. So, naturally, that's where I worked. I now realize that one of the last 'jobs' I had there presaged the project management work I now do in my professional career: the expediter.

Those of you who have logged hours in restaurants on the eating side of things may or may not know how it all works where the magic happens, so here's the short version: there is the back of house staff who stay in the kitchen where they cook and prep; and there is the front of house staff, comprised of waiters, waitresses, and hostesses, who talk to the people who come in (that's you). There are but two parties who negotiate both worlds: the bus staff, who have a perilous but relatively well defined mission— travel from the front of the house to the back with dirty dishes; and the expediter. The expediter manages the flow of traffic: timing the orders, prepping plates for delivery, and serving as a mediator between the cooks and the wait staff. For example:

> No, that can't be prepared on the side.
> OK, we can hold this appetizer for the dinner course.
> Where is that fish?
> No, I don't care how famous your table is they can't come into the kitchen and look at the oven in person.
> Wait, that plate needs parsley.
> Yes, you are right, that fish should already be done; let me make sure they get a free dessert.

This person often stands at the a window or entrance to the kitchen and so has a view of the whole operation. The expediter is not the manager and has no inherent overarching authority, but s/he in many ways sets the tone for the rhythm of how the work gets done. Everybody wants the same thing—good food, delivered on time, a pleasant experience for all involved—but the different groups often have trouble visualizing what the other goes through to get to that agreed-upon destination. This is where the expediter helps out by serving as the bridge.

It was only when I got into project management that I began to see the parallels between my time in the kitchen and my time in application development. Less routine use of knives in the latter than the former, obviously, but still back of house staff (coders) and front of house staff (non-coders, librarians or otherwise) and a need for someone to **translate**.

At some points in a project, you definitely want everyone at the table together to talk—but even then, keep your ears pricked for incompatible dialects. After all, some say "reference" and some say 01110010 01100101 01100110 01100101 01110010 01100101 01101110 01100011 01100101[36]

Enter you to save the day, speaking geek to the geeks and referencing reference with the reference librarians and chatting circ with the circulation folks ... and you get the idea. Rephrase to ensure understanding ("Let me just be sure I am following—I think we agreed to ...").

A final observation on project management: there is one more method of translation that you will need to master, and that is writing project requirements and/or specifications. Learn how to write good requirements if you are going to be working on tech projects; it will be a time saver, a money saver and a morale saver. I would hope that nobody would dream of starting the construction of a building by saying, "Well, we have that stained glass window we wanted to use so we've slapped up some framing and installed that. See? There it is. Now can you pour the foundations, and do all the plumbing and power

---

36. Whee! You can trot out this party trick also: http://www.binaryhexconverter.com/ascii-text-to-binary-converter

and all that other stuff like walls and whatever. Let us know when you are done." Yet the functional equivalent of this happens all the time in software projects. Specifications and requirements are the blueprints for your project; they are also kind of like a contract between you and the development team so they and you both can feel certain they are building what you intend.

INVESTIGATE

The trouble with translation is that there are so many ways to interpret it! Below find three—literal translation of your site into another language; turning ideas into software requirements, and a few things just to get you started on project management, which is a long-term study unto itself.

Fagan, Jody Condit, and Jennifer A. Keach. 2009. *Web Project Management for Academic Libraries*. Oxford: Chandos.

LeFeuvre, Antoine. 2012. "Translation Is UX." *A List Apart*, December 2. http://alistapart.com/article/translation-is-ux.

Ponce, Ron. 2009. "Project Management: 8 Steps to On-Time, On-Budget Delivery." *CIO*, May 20. http://www.cio.com/article/493128/Project_Management_8_Steps_to_On_Time_On_Budget_Delivery.

Revels, Ira. 2010. "Managing Digital Projects." *American Libraries*, March 10. http://www.americanlibrariesmagazine.org/article/managing-digital-projects.

Rinzler, Ben. 2009. *Telling Stories: A Short Path to Writing Better Software Requirements*. Indianapolis, IN: Wiley Pub., Inc.

#19 Polish

Gone are the days when the internet was full of pages sporting bold yellow text on purple, or giant background images of broccoli or butterflies, or that little guy endlessly digging, digging. Well, perhaps he's not entirely gone—but we will not acknowledge such realities here.

The fact is that even our least tech-savvy populations have come to expect high-quality interfaces, fonts that always read properly, no unseemly displays of error codes or gobble-dygook from databases, sites that can be viewed from any device, icons that look professional, buttons that work and forms that send. In other words, they expect your site to function without failing and they expect it to look pretty darn good doing it.

For libraries, the stakes are high. There are lots of easier places to go to do research on the web and a good number of these places (Google, I'm looking at you) have huge budgets for user interface design and such. This means that it's worth our time to **polish** up what we do before we put it out there in the world. Double and triple check for typos. Make sure all the sides are even. Check to make sure the door swipe works. Take the time to adjust by a pixel or two to get it just right. Don't roll your own if you can use a well-established convention or code library (JQuery Mobile[37], for example) that presents your information in the way that users will have come to expect in their interactions with the 'regular' web. Investigate what icon sets are freely available for non-commercial use. Comply with brand standards for your college or university.

That said, before I whip you into a perfectionistic freak-out attack, let me conclude by contradicting the advice I just gave and encouraging you to loosen up. Yes, these things are important; yes, people rely on our services and resources to do their work; yes, it matters

---

37. http://jquerymobile.com/

that they are functional and professional. But all of this polish work can be taken too far and become a blocker to action. Many times the only way you will ever really know how something works out in the field and whether the users take to it is... to put it out there in the field and see whether the users take to it. Slap the word 'beta' on it if so doing makes you feel better, but after you have done what you can, i.e. ensured that the Dean's name is spelled correctly, the signage points the right way and all the links resolve, set your project free and let it try its wings.

We know that the research process is iterative—we start with an idea; collect information; evaluate what we find for scope, value, depth; possibly adjust the focus of the topic, then cycle back through. A research topic is in fact a hypothesis, and we test it through data gathering and measuring the results, then possibly revise our hypothesis. There's a concept called the 'minimum viable product' that applies this same sort of process to software development, relying on what's called a "build-measure-learn feedback loop."[38] *Minimum viable product* isn't the first junky old thing that works at all and then you fling it at people and hope it sticks, it's "that version of a new product which allows a team to collect the maximum amount of validated learning about customers with the least effort."[39]

Our services and resources are meant to be used. We hire people to help other people find and make use of the things we buy and build. An empty building or an unvisited website makes no sound in the forest. Unlike our monograph collections, our services and websites don't have fixed editions. Though we rarely exercise it, we have the freedom to make changes on the fly. Libraries serve large, diverse groups and somebody out there is going to find the needle in the haystack, or present an edge case you never could've thought of ahead of time, and you'll just have to solve it as it arises—this is what 'validated learning' means in the quote above.

Do your best and put it out there. It'll be great. And if it's not, you can fix it.

---

38. The Lean Startup, "Methodology."
39. Ries, "Lessons Learned."

INVESTIGATE

In this reading list, I'm including three books written by successful entrepreneurs (seems to me that requires a good balance between polishing & loosening up), and the house blog for 37signals, the company founded by Jason Fried & David Heinemeier Hansson and known for the popular project management product Basecamp.

On the topic of feedback loops, **#7 Sift**, **#8 Ask** and **#17 Listen** might be helpful to review as well.

Basecamp. 2014. *Signal Vs. Noise—Business, Design, Programming and the Web*. Accessed April 25. https://signalvnoise.com/.

37signals (Firm). 2006. *Getting Real: The Smarter, Faster, Easier Way to Build a Successful Web Application*. [Chicago, IL]: 37signals.

Fried, Jason, and David Heinemeier Hansson. 2010. *Rework*. New York: Crown Business.

Ries, Eric. 2011. *The Lean Startup: How Today's Entrepreneurs Use Continuous Innovation to Create Radically Successful Businesses*. New York: Crown Business.

#20 Test

Since this chapter is about testing, why not start with a quick quiz.

Usability testing:
- A) Must be undertaken by licensed experts, costs a lot, and takes forever.
- B) Can require a (sometimes long and painful) human subjects review process.
- C) Gives you a chance to view your users in action, completing tasks you'd like to observe.
- D) Really just requires a bit of planning, a little organization and a lot of curiosity.
- E) A and B.
- F) B, C, D.
- G) C and D.
- H) Wow this is a long quiz and I forgot what we were talking about.

Even though some people might have been tempted to choose *E) A and B*, the answer is actually *F) B, C, D*. [You can see that I am striving to be honest because if I weren't I would be suggesting the answer was *G) C and D*. If you answered *H)*, it might be time to once again take a moment to read **#10 Escape** again and come back to this later on.]

So, to recap, usability testing:
- *Can require a (sometimes long and painful) human subjects review process.*
  If you think you might want to share or publish your results, or think you might ever use them for anything other than internal discussion within your department,

I suggest you bite the bullet and go through the human subjects review process at your institution. In fact, I'd further suggest that you ask around to get a sense of the culture around this at your place of work—at some colleges and universities, any testing at all, even fairly informal testing, really needs to go through this process and you don't want to be out of compliance.

- *Gives you a chance to view your users in action, completing tasks you'd like to observe.* Yes, you can be fancier and you can calculate all sorts of statistics, but—the essence of a usability **test** is this: watching folks complete specific tasks of interest and seeing how it goes.

- *Really just requires a bit of planning, a little organization and a lot of curiosity.* The more people are involved, the more planning you need, mostly just because you want all the test participants to have the same experience and in order to guarantee that, all your testers need to be on the same page as far as process. But it really is pretty simple. You can start with really common tasks you know lots of people do; you can start with tasks that you suspect have workflow problems; you can start with processes that are brand new additions, or even test ideas that you've been mulling over to see if they work at all in the real world. Do those tasks yourself to get a sense of what you'd define as the 'Expert Path.' Then bring some folks in and ask them to do the tasks. There you are.

It's really all about levels of testing—sure, sometimes you will want to do a large scale test that requires significant planning, budget and data analysis. But other times you might just want to know how the first five people to stop by your table in the student union feel about your new button. The key idea I would like to get across here is that usability testing is really best thought of as something that emerges from a culture, rather than a single discrete project or even a series of events.

Are you curious? Can you make notes? Do you have a place, any place, where you can bring in members of your user group and ask them to click around on a web page or point at things on a paper prototype? Then you are ready to start testing.

INVESTIGATE

There are plenty of great books about usability testing that you can look through to help you with methods. Here are a few favorite titles that have long been part of my professional bookshelf. I cut my usability testing teeth on these so they're great for beginners; but I still go back and refer to them, so I think there's something in them for more advanced testers as well.

Krug, Steve. 2006. *Don't Make Me Think!: a Common Sense Approach to Web Usability*. Berkeley, CA: New Riders Pub.

——. 2010. *Rocket Surgery Made Easy: The Do-it-yourself Guide to Finding and Fixing Usability Problems*. Berkeley, CA.: New Riders.

Rubin, Jeffrey. 2008. *Handbook of Usability Testing How to Plan, Design, and Conduct Effective Tests*. Indianapolis, IN: Wiley Pub.

#21 Fail—Cheerfully!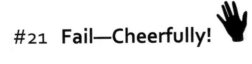

"If Ernest Hemingway, James Michener, Neil Simon, Frank Lloyd Wright, and Pablo Picasso could not get it right the first time, what makes you think that you will?"
—Paul Heckel

We are now at the half-way point in the book, so I feel like we know each other well enough for me to ask you a really personal question. Are you ready? (No, that wasn't the question.) Here goes:

Have you failed? Recently? Ever?

Like, really, really, really blew it.

OK, I'll go first. Now, I am not talking about those little garden-variety goofs that pile up over the years and get to be hard to remember, like showing up on the wrong day for a meeting, or forgetting your weekend reference desk shift, or filing the papers wrong, or letting your mouth blurt something out before your brain was finished thinking. Those could happen to anyone—it's called being human and making mistakes. Which sometimes can also be the makings of a big fail: for example, I broke the library website once. I found out that it was broken during a meeting—about the library website, how's that for meta—and didn't even connect what I had done to the outage until later on when one of our developers told me, surreptitiously, what had really happened. I had been making a quick change to the production server (fail one: always make changes in test, then move to production) when the phone rang, I got distracted, and left out a bracket (fail two: keep your mind on what you are doing). Then, I blithely submitted the changes (see fail one) and took off to said meeting (fail three: validate to see that everything works before moving on). So, when I found out that it was in fact my missing bracket that was responsible, I decided I'd better face it head-on. I picked up the phone, called the library director, and told her what happened. Our colleagues in IT had been gracious enough not to point fingers at me, so I felt the only grown-up thing to do was to set the record straight lest their reluctance to share details cause blame to be assigned to them. Was it a fun phone call? Well, no. But it was a fine phone call, and I am still here to tell you about it.

That, admittedly, was a fairly benign public personal fail, in that the whole thing happened and was wrapped up within two hours on a quiet Friday afternoon. It could have been much worse—one could lose a boatload of money, find oneself up a creek from trusting the wrong person or company, make a miscalculation and lose one's job. Then there are what I think of as the intrinsic fails: lying, cheating, stealing, etc., and getting caught (a double fail). Yes, sometimes failure leads to serious consequences. But a lot of the time, it just martyrs our egos and fills us full of humble pie. Neither of those things has ever killed anyone, although your ego will try and tell you otherwise.

Here's the part where some folks are smugly shaking their heads at my confession and thinking to themselves they have never and will never do anything like that. Well, maybe not exactly like that but—get out your fork, I've got a plate of pie for you: If you haven't failed you aren't trying enough things, you're lying, or you are deluded. Maybe all three at once.[40]

Excellence requires growth. Growth requires learning. Learning requires change—changing what information we have, how we think, what we think, how we do things, sometimes even who we are. Change is inextricably imbued with risk. Risk, by definition, implies that failure is possible, if not likely. Doing something great isn't safe and it isn't easy. Doing something good might not be either. Great and good frontload the risk. I do want to insert this cautionary note lest I be misunderstood: I am not celebrating failure for failure's sake.

---

40. P.S. You have definitely failed. It's ok.

Going out unprepared and intending to fail is stupid, careless and sloppy and I am 100% against it. It's costly in terms of time, money, morale and reputation.

That said, nothing ventured, nothing gained. Hearing stories of other people's attempts, their failures, their analysis of where things went wrong and the takeaways they gleaned from the experience is very helpful and the panels of this sort that have been springing up at library conferences are an interesting development.[41]

INVESTIGATE

Since we just had dessert, I won't fill you up right now with inspiring stories of invention, breakthrough, and perseverance—just think of your personal favorites. I myself am partial to thinking about Abraham Lincoln. But, if you get hungry later, here are some good snacks.

Crawford, Amy. 2013. "Why the Best Success Stories Often Begin With Failure." *Smithsonian*, February.

Enis, Matt. 2013. "Fail4Lib: Problematic Projects Generate Constructive Conversation." *Library Journal*. http://lj.libraryjournal.com/2013/03/technology/fail4lib-problematic-projects-generate-constructive-conversation/.

Harford, Tim. 2011. *Adapt: Why Success Always Starts with Failure*. 1st ed. New York: Farrar, Straus and Giroux.

White, Erin R. 2014. "What I Mean When I Say 'fail Open.'" *Erin R. White*. http://erinrwhite.com/what-i-mean-when-i-say-fail-open/.

---

41.   One example is the recent fail4lib Pre-Conference prior to the 2013 code4lib conference in Chicago; read about it in the *Library Journal* write-up, referenced in the notes at the end of this section.

#22 Raid $⚙

I am not talking about a stealthy lunchtime operation aimed at the box of doughnuts in the department across the hall. (Although, if doughnuts can survive all morning and into lunch in your workplace, I applaud you for your self-discipline and healthy ways.)

As mentioned in a previous point, iterative testing is a cultural thing and it can happen at a number of levels. Here we consider the guerilla approach.

Most people who've worked in an academic library for any length of time would agree with the statement that undergraduates are easily susceptible to offers of food. So bank on that. It's very simple.

1. Think of a single task you'd like to review. Don't make it too complicated.
   Good examples: Renew your books. Find the hours for a certain library. Access JSTOR. Look for a research guide on the topic of a class you are taking right now. Search for articles on X topic in this here database I already have open and ready for you and tell me what you think of how it looks and works. Text yourself a call number from this search results set and tell me if you think that works well. Use your smartphone to access the library mobile site URL and perform some specific function on the mobile site.
   Bad example: Come up with a topic, choose a database, find an article, and save it to a list. [This task, while interesting and useful to investigate, is a bit more complex. It also measures things that may be outside the scope of how well your site performs—choose a topic—so in my humble opinion, dropping the first part about the topic would make it a task more appropriate for a more structured, formal usability test. Either way, definitely not suitable for a drive-by test in a busy, noisy space.]

2. (optional) Write up a very, very short survey to go with said tasks covering details like gender, status (undergraduate/what year, graduate, faculty), major or department, etc. Preferably this should be no more than five questions and should be able to be completed in two minutes or less with minimal cognitive load. If you choose to do this, you can use this later to figure out how representative (or not) your convenience sample was.

3. Identify a high-traffic area where you can set up with a laptop, tablet, or clipboard for an hour or two.

4. (optional) Make some simple signage. I have had pretty good success with using an iPad to display a PDF that says something like 'Help Us Test: 5 minutes or less.' We were surprised at how many people were simply drawn to the table by the tablet computer.

5. Arm yourself with candy or granola bars (some folks will notice these even more than a tablet).

6. Go forth.

You may be surprised at the number of graduate students you lure with this technique. I have found most faculty members seem to be able to resist the candy bars but that may vary by campus—I generally proactively recruit faculty via email, rather than relying on this more scattershot approach. That said, if there is an orientation or colloquium where you can set up shop in the foyer, you might be able to employ a version of this approach with a faculty group. If you fear they won't want to be seen eating candy, give out bookmarks or jump drives.

True, this kind of usability **raid** isn't going to give you statistically significant results, but it can reveal opportunities for big wins from small changes, give you a sense of whether you are barking up the wrong tree entirely with contemplated changes, and provide valuable insights in the form of off-the-cuff comments and initial reactions from the people who stop by. All of this for the low, low price of a few candy bars (or granola bars for the health-conscious)—and if you really want to broaden your reach, be extra considerate and provide the option of vegan or gluten-free snacks like tiny bags of nuts. People will appreciate your thoughtfulness. You will appreciate their feedback. Everybody wins.

#23 Anticipate

Even the most dedicated UX librarian could fall victim to jargon deafness ("I don't under-stand why I get so many puzzled looks when I tell my freshman orientation group about serial monographs") and UI blindness ("it's so easy, you just scroll down, click here, click over there, fill out a form, submit and then click again!") at any time. Generally, though, it's safe to say that there are many things within our libraries that we already know are confusing.

This one is simple—**anticipate** those confusions. Where possible, solve problems for your users before they even have them. If you can, fix them. If you can't fix them—because it's a vendor interface, or you don't own the service, or you can't rebuild your building, or what-have-you—then seek to mitigate that sticky wicket.

Sometimes this is really specific: I read once about a library that charged patrons to check out certain types of movies. Sometimes there would be problems with the physical items themselves—didn't work, mangled tape, etc. In those cases the patron would want their money back, but it was complicated and time-consuming for the person at the desk to either credit the account or refund the cash. Even though it was only $1.50 per movie, this resulted in a lot of bad feelings. Their solution: provide a coupon for a free "rental." No cash changed hands, the patrons felt satisfied, less stress on the desk staffers. Problem solved.[42]

Recently we eliminated a common point of confusion in our catalog related to the items from our dorm libraries—they're popular, they're recent, they only circulate to dorm residents, and we couldn't make them non-requestable through regular means due to some workflow issues. This meant any user could go all the way through the request process only to receive an opaque error message at the last step. This was clearly not cool. So, we simply suppressed the request button for items in the affected group of locations. Even-

---

42. Turner, "Dealing with Angry People," 51.

tually we'll need to address the underlying workflow issue, but in the meantime, we've at least eliminated some frustration for our patrons.

Other times it might be a more general response. A couple of years ago, we took a look at our 404 error page, which is the page that someone gets when they enter a URL for our website that can't be retrieved (it might be a deleted page, simply incorrect or misspelled, etc.). We reasoned to ourselves that nobody goes to a 404 error page on purpose, except nerds like ourselves who are testing or reviewing them, so why not offer a glimmer of hope and help there in the form of an IM reference widget? That way anyone who found themselves at an error page would quickly be able to get real answers from a real person during the many hours we staff IM reference. Our logs don't show that we get much traffic from that source, but we feel good knowing that even for those few times someone stumbled onto that page, we were there to help.

Can you reword some signage? Perhaps add or remove some signage? Simplify a process? Make a bookmark with a human-readable shortcut URL for that one thing everyone has to do on your site that is really hard to find, but can't be moved?

CONTEMPLATE

Go back to the notes you made for **#4 Notice**. This would be a great place to take some action on those. Or, do some thinking about your 404 page:

Miller, Brad. 2013. "404 Page Best Practices." *Search Engine Watch*. http://searchenginewatch.com/article/2293339/404-Page-Best-Practices.
Waisburg, Daniel. 2013. "Monitoring & Analyzing Error Pages (404s) Using Analytics." *Google Analytics Blog*. http://analytics.blogspot.com/2013/09/monitoring-analyzing-error-pages-404s.html.

#24 Smile 🕐 ✋

"Whenever you want to tap into a superpower that will help you and everyone around you live a longer, healthier, happier life—smile."
—Ron Gutman, TED 2011[43]

This one is really so easy and will get you so far. Truth: You don't have to feel overwhelmingly, soul-shatteringly happy to manage a smile. Do you feel like going to work every day? I sure don't. Do you go? I thought so. (Me too.)

I'm not going to summarize for you the numerous scientific studies about how smiling lengthens your life, improves relationships, makes you more approachable, and is generally beneficial to you and everybody else too—you will enjoy hearing Ron Gutman's excellent TED talk a lot more (and it's only seven minutes long—check the references at the end of this session).

Dare to smile at people. Despite the load of tripe we've been fed all our lives by the Scholarly Industrial Complex, and the How To Be Cool Brigade, being professional and having fun don't have to be mutually exclusive. It has often seemed to me, in my unscientific observations over the years, that looking somber or dour is sometimes perceived as deeper, more "scholarly," or more "responsible." I mostly wonder if those terminally serious people can be feeling 100% well, or if their shoes pinch, or maybe they are doing extremely complicated math in their heads.

As I get older I find that I am increasingly more happy all the time, but then I've learned to work at it; and I've learned how to find a smile even when I find I really truly can't turn on the happy faucet. I think about the many people at the many service desks I visit as a customer and how much easier and more pleasant it is for me when they start our interac-

---

43. *Ron Gutman: The Hidden Power of Smiling.*

tion with a smile. Occasionally I just have to slap myself around and cling to thinking about how grateful I am to have easy access to modern plumbing, or how I'm totally going to take a nap when I get home. Just like running a marathon, or finishing a degree, or achieving anything worth achieving—you have to want it. Sometimes you have to take one for the team, and that can mean managing to muster up a tiny happy thought that results in a smile and a pleasant greeting to your colleagues and the people you serve ... when you'd really rather just slug the world in the jaw. Bottom line: smiling does not actually require being happy, although it can create conditions favorable to an improved mood.

Remember: the goal here is a great user experience, and the easiest way to start that is with a smile. Nobody's asking you to promise to be happy forever, or never have a bad day, or to diminish the seriousness of your student loans or a family health situation, or relinquish your extremely valid concerns about the environment or the state of the world—but it sure can make for a better customer service interaction if you temporarily back-burner that stuff when you are working with the public and interacting with your colleagues.

INVESTIGATE

I recognize this can be challenging! So, as a librarian, my natural reaction is to provide a reading and viewing list, as a bibliography makes everything better.

Gutman, Ron. "Ron Gutman: The Hidden Power of Smiling." Filmed March 2011. TED video, 7:26. Posted May 2011. http://www.ted.com/talks/ron_gutman_the_hidden_power_of_smiling.html.

Spector, Robert. 2005. *The Nordstrom Way to Customer Service Excellence: a Handbook for Implementing Great Service in Your Organization*. Hoboken, N.J: John Wiley & Sons.

Weinzweig, Ari, and Zingermans (Restaurant). 2004. *Zingerman's Guide to Giving Great Service*. 1st hardcover ed. New York, NY: Hyperion.

#25 Defuse

Figure 2: Dynamite, Sean MacEntee (Flickr)

Try to say nothing negative about anybody for three days, for forty-five days, for three months. See what happens to your life.
—Yoko Ono[44]

We never really "did" Lent growing up, but after several years working at a Catholic university, I thought I'd give it a try—so, one year, I gave up complaining. This went about as well as you can imagine, as far as my ability to stick to it for sustained periods of time, but it was still one of the most useful exercises I've ever undertaken. As it happened, a colleague of mine gave up criticism that same year. It was a happy coincidence of timing for us and served as an amazing support group. We'd find ourselves in each other's offices

44.   Yoko Ono , Microblog, @yokoono, July 22, 2011.

pretty frequently, saying, "There's so much I CAN'T SAY right now!! Talk me down!"

Back to Yoko and her tweet: negativity and blame are like cancer, a pair of toxic twins. They are unnecessary and unproductive. They're ugly. And they breed. Don't do it—to your patrons, to your coworkers. It's not going to fix anything. It's going to create an unpleasant atmosphere in the workplace which is going to eke out into your public-facing areas. This is a user experience killer.

Why do we do this? I'm sure the reasons could be many and varied. Let me give you something to consider about why this might happen and the impact it can have:

> Our research shows that people believe they will appear smarter to their bosses if they are more critical—and it often works. In many organizations, it is professionally rewarding to react critically to new ideas. Unfortunately, this sort of negativity bias can have severe consequences for the creativity of those being evaluated ... such a culture creates a climate of fear, which again undermines intrinsic motivation.[45]

I don't know about you, but that does not sound like something I want to participate in.

You don't sit around and talk about a bomb, do you? You don't consider its motivations and gripe about how loudly it ticks. You just **defuse** the thing before it blows up. So, similarly, seek to eliminate unnecessary points of conflict. If there is a problem to be addressed, by all means address it: directly, unemotionally, constructively. So often we complain about things that aren't in our realm of responsibility or authority. I have a series of three questions I started asking myself a few years ago and they've dramatically improved my mood:

- How important is this, really? Truly important or just something someone does differently than me?
- Can I do something about it? Or can I say something and then let it drop?

---

45. Amabile, "How to Kill Creativity," 83.

- And finally, do I need to have an opinion about this? Like, really *need* to have one? If no, then don't.

It has resulted in an amazing savings of time and energy.

One final note to consider: the "toxic twins" are bad enough aimed outwardly, but I've also been thinking a lot about how it's impossible to judge or criticize other people without doing the same to yourself—once you activate that lens, whether you realize it or not, you are bringing that same harshness to everything. The knife cuts both ways. Complaining and criticizing feed on themselves and then turn on you. Sometimes you can see it right away, or as you ignore it, it builds up and burbles into a toxic mess that will eventually either poison you from the inside or, like dynamite, suddenly become unstable and combust, usually at the worst possible moment. And really, is there a good moment for a toxic explosion? I'm going to say no. So just snip the green wire and be done with it. Or, wait—was it the red wire?

INVESTIGATE

Baas, Matthijs, Carsten K. W. De Dreu, and Bernard A. Nijstad. 2011. "Creative Production by Angry People Peaks Early On, Decreases over Time, and Is Relatively Unstructured." *Journal of Experimental Social Psychology* 47 (6): 1107–15. doi:10.1016/j.jesp.2011.05.009.
On the topic of the negative impact of criticism in the workplace: This article is quite interesting, but if you don't have time to read it, the authors' helpfully long and descriptive title delivers the main take-away. Yes, raging against the machine in a toxic environment might briefly pump up your creative output, but in the long run, it's something to avoid.

Kahn, Jonathan. 2014. "People Skills for Web Workers." *A List Apart*, March 25. http://
     alistapart.com/article/people-skills-for-web-workers.
Stone, Douglas. 2010. *Difficult Conversations: How to Discuss What Matters Most.* 10th
     anniversary ed., [2nd ed.]. New York: Penguin Books.
     In addition to giving some thought to the series of three questions I out-
     lined above, I've found this book's insights to be helpful when thinking
     about when it might be helpful to take the bull by the horns and ask a ques-
     tion, or conversely, to acknowledge when the issue is really on my side and
     I maybe need to let it go—or apologize.

#26 Sketch

Why is this workflow so difficult? How best to express this? Where should we put that? What would be the clearest way to explain or lay out some process?

A lot of what we do is visual—certainly our web sites, definitely our signage and our buildings, and even our workflows, too, whether we think about them that way or not.

Often, though, these are the sorts of discussions that can quickly become pretty frustrating and wind up in an endless loop of one person saying, "No, no—arranged more like X?" and the other person saying, "Oh! Like Y."

Some things you can't just talk through, either because your words haven't caught up with your brain ("You know, like, if they could just SEE the stuff? On the left? By the thingie? No, the other thingie!"), or because what you are talking about is more spatially-oriented (A: "If we moved the sofa and then the table and then switched the direction, it would all fit!" B: "..."), or because you are talking about a process where something happens and then things change and something else happens. You might not be able to talk about something because you are 100% totally stuck and your mind feels blank.

This calls for drawing. For starters, it's kind of fun; and more to the point, it's non-verbal. There's a great deal of empirical evidence that suggests that one hemisphere of the brain tends to specialize in analytical, verbal, sequential thought and that the other hemisphere tends toward processing that is "rapid, complex, whole-pattern, spatial and perceptual."[46] This latter is the sort of thinking that can lead to the "A-ha!" moment. In short, drawing can let the wordless side of your brain have a go. It can be easier to *see*

---

46. Edwards, *The New Drawing on the Right Side of the Brain*, 33.

a problem in a diagram than to *say* a problem. We've probably all had the experience of trying to give someone directions, watching them become ever more lengthy when written out, then switching gears and drawing a simple, understandable map in seconds.

You don't have to be Picasso and you don't even have to be good at all. You just have to grab a pen or a pencil or a dry erase marker and start making some marks with it. These efforts can be very low fidelity—think cocktail napkin and marker—or high fidelity, like finished design comps. You can draw a bunch of boxes and arrows on a whiteboard to help you think through a process. You can rough out a bunch of rectangles on a waste sheet of paper to help you put the big pieces of a web page together right, or figure the right angle for that new soft seating. Whatever you do, just pick up something and **sketch**. It's a start, not a finish, and focusing on this in-process, messy thinking can get you un-stuck, or spark a whole new way of looking at things. Betty Edwards, author of *Drawing on the Right Side of the Brain*, points out how useful it can be to all kinds of problem solving to shift gears:

> At least part, and perhaps much of what we see is changed, interpreted, or conceptualized in ways that depend on a person's training, mind-set, and past experiences. We tend to see what we expect to see or what we decide we have seen. This expectation or decision, however, often is not a conscious process. Instead, the brain frequently does the expecting and the deciding, without our conscious awareness, and then alters or rearranges—or even simply disregards –the raw data of vision that hits the retina. Learning perception through drawing seems to change this process and to allow a different, more direct kind of seeing. The brain's editing is somehow put on hold, thereby permitting one to see more fully and perhaps more realistically.[47]

A picture is worth a thousand words! Start your sketching, ladies and gentlemen.

---

47. Ibid., xxv.

INVESTIGATE

Below find some resources I've found exceptionally helpful—and do yourself a favor and get *Drawing on the Right Side of the Brain*. It's truly transformative, and full of interesting info that will shift your perspective.

Buxton, William. 2007. *Sketching User Experience: Getting the Design Right and the Right Design*. San Francisco: Morgan Kaufmann.

Cheng, Kevin. 2013. "See What I Mean." *A List Apart*, February 26. http://alistapart.com/article/see-what-i-mean.

Edwards, Betty. 1999. *The New Drawing on the Right Side of the Brain*. 2nd rev. ed. New York: Jeremy P. Tarcher/Putnam.

Follett, Jonathan. 2009. "A Practical Guide to Capturing Creativity for UX." *UX Matters*. http://www.uxmatters.com/mt/archives/2009/07/a-practical-guide-to-capturing-creativity-for-ux.php.

Some of what you will find in the following is helpful, and some not, but I'm pretty confident if you browse this Flickr group (organized around UX sketches) a bit you'll find something interesting: http://www.flickr.com/groups/uxsketches/

#27 Engage

If you were fortunate enough to hear Ira Glass give the closing keynote for the ACRL National Conference in 2009 about the power of narrative you probably remember it—because, naturally, he managed to construct a great narrative through which to deliver his talk ... about great narrative. It was very meta, and very funny, and at my former place of work we went right back and worked up an at-home workshop about the power of narrative in teaching, complete with props for all who attended (heavy-framed black eyeglasses *of course*).

Ira Glass is known for his heavy-framed black eyeglasses and hoodie sweatshirt, and for being the host and executive producer of the tremendously successful *This American Life.* It is rather mildly described on its website as "a weekly public radio show ... mostly true stories of everyday people, though not always."[48] (Although they do allow themselves to mention that they've "won all the major broadcasting awards.") As evidenced by the show's general acclaim from listeners and critics, Ira Glass is a man who understands the power of how a well-crafted story can draw the listener in and forge connections, because, as he pointed out in the aforementioned ACRL talk, we are wired to interpret our experiences as a narrative.

And yes, there's some science to why storytelling affects people so strongly:

> Not only are the language processing parts in our brain activated, but any other area in our brain that we would use when experiencing the events of the story are too. If someone tells us about how delicious certain foods were, our sensory cortex lights up ... When we tell stories to others that have really helped us shape our thinking and way of life, we can have the same effect on them too.[49]

---

48. Chicago Public Media, "About Us."
49. Widrich, "The Science of Storytelling."

Before you start thinking, *Hold on there Svengali, I want to help people, not flim-flam them into buying a bridge*, consider this thought from Malcolm Gladwell, another tremendously engaging communicator whose medium happens to be writing: "Good writing does not succeed or fail on the strength of its ability to persuade ... It succeeds or fails on the strength of its ability to **engage** you, to make you think, to give you a glimpse into someone else's head—even if in the end you conclude that someone else's head is not a place you'd really like to be."[50]

What does this mean for UX work? Your role as UX practitioner is to find the story that needs to be told, and to tell it in an engaging way. The story of how to find a peer-reviewed journal article might not be quite as compelling to some as a story about why the academy strives for excellence in its pursuit of knowledge. (Yes, I do realize that that second story is not always suited for the reference desk; but I submit to you that banker's lamps in a reading room seem to put people in mind of that second narrative and *that* is part of why that kind of study space is generally very popular.)

A good user experience requires a strong narrative: first and foremost, for your end-users as you present information, contextual clues, emphasis, and the somewhat ephemeral (though powerful) aesthetic quality that shapes their experience with your building, your website, your services.

Even before that, narrative comes into play behind the scenes with your colleagues and co-constructors, as you work to craft that public experience with what Gabrielle Dolan and Yamini Naidu call a business story. What does this mean? "Business storytelling is different from traditional storytelling because in business your stories have a purpose; are supported by data; and are authentic, true stories that relate back to your purpose."[51] Hmm, sounds very similar to the outcomes of many user-centered design methodologies

---

50. Gladwell, *What the Dog Saw and Other Adventures*, xv.
51. Dolan and Naidu, *Hooked*, 6.

to me. In their well-known book *Made to Stick*, Chip and Dan Heath make a comment that's useful to consider in relation to business storytelling:

> The story's power ... is twofold: It provides simulation (knowledge about how to act) and inspiration (motivation to act). Note that both benefits, simulation and inspiration, are geared to generating *action*.... A *credible* idea makes people believe. An *emotional* idea makes people care. ... The right stories make people act.[52]

One final note: A powerful story is also an appropriately timed story; nobody wants to hear in-depth information about using archival collections (*yet*) when they can't find the door to the building.

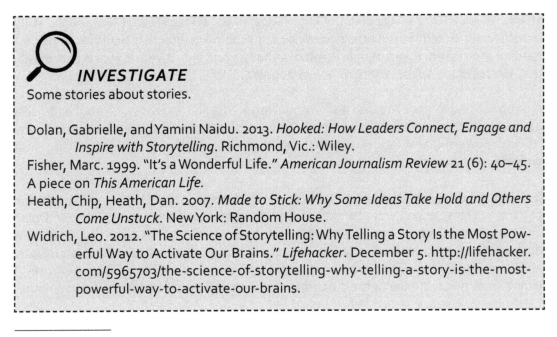

INVESTIGATE
Some stories about stories.

Dolan, Gabrielle, and Yamini Naidu. 2013. *Hooked: How Leaders Connect, Engage and Inspire with Storytelling*. Richmond, Vic.: Wiley.
Fisher, Marc. 1999. "It's a Wonderful Life." *American Journalism Review* 21 (6): 40–45. A piece on *This American Life*.
Heath, Chip, Heath, Dan. 2007. *Made to Stick: Why Some Ideas Take Hold and Others Come Unstuck*. New York: Random House.
Widrich, Leo. 2012. "The Science of Storytelling: Why Telling a Story Is the Most Powerful Way to Activate Our Brains." *Lifehacker*. December 5. http://lifehacker. com/5965703/the-science-of-storytelling-why-telling-a-story-is-the-most-powerful-way-to-activate-our-brains.

---

52. Heath, *Made to Stick*, 206.

#28 Play

Hitting the wall—it happens to everyone. There are little tiny walls many of us hit on a relatively frequent basis, generally somewhere around three in the afternoon; those are fairly responsive to a five-minute stretch break, a cup of coffee, a little snack, or a quick walk around the block.

Then there are those times when a figurative Great Wall of China appears between you and doing whatever it is that you need to accomplish: coming up with that new idea, wrapping up that last tricky piece of the project, trying to re-think an old system or think up a new system, solving a seemingly unsolvable problem, dreaming the impossible dream (more on that later). What to do, if you can't just flee the building for a reset (see **#10 Escape**)?

I can still recall the frisson of excitement that went across the internet when articles started popping up about "20 % time": "Google employees can work on whatever they want for 20% of their time!!" This clearly sounded too good to be true (and as expressed in the previous sentence, it was), but the truth was still pretty good: "Google engineers are encouraged to take 20 percent of their time to work on something company-related that interests them personally."[53] Some of these innovations turned out to be extremely successful, like Gmail; others surely never have seen the light of day. In her seminal article "How to Kill Creativity" Teresa M. Amabile points out, "In business, originality isn't enough. To be creative, an idea must also be appropriate—useful and actionable. It must somehow influence the way business gets done—by improving a product, for instance, or by opening up a new way to approach a process."[54]

---

53. Mediratta, "The Google Way."
54. Amabile, "How to Kill Creativity," 78.

The much touted "Google 20%" project might not be feasible for you and your workplace, but creating some space in your schedule to let your brain breathe and to try out new things is actually a pretty savvy way of upping your productivity. When you are feeling worn out or otherwise backed into a corner, sometimes the best thing you can do at work is **play**.

Trying out new things just to play gives you space to think about how it might work for libraries later. Or maybe not! Maybe it's mostly just fun, but a little bit handy in that now you have a better handle on Zotero, or apps for research on a smartphone, or working with data feeds. Perhaps the outcome of your work-play is a really great display in the lobby, or some interesting survey data.

It might add up to improved morale—like the short skit penned in the late 1970s about library research, recently discovered in a collection of items about our library's history, gloriously and hilariously staged by staff on the project team. More than just morale, fun can increase output, and even quality of output: "Cultivating an environment that allows for playfulness and is positively building ... quiets the voice of unhealthy perfectionism and embraces healthy perfectionism."[55]

The key here is balance. Research & development isn't the primary function of most people's jobs, and even Google only allows employees a maximum of a day a week working on their pet projects. A little time thinking about a new or different problem can re-energize your practice; lose the right proportion and you risk being, or seeming, distracted and unproductive. Along these lines, Amabile notes:

> ...plodding through long dry spells of tedious experimentation increases the probability of truly creative breakthroughs. So, too, does a work style that uses 'incubation,' the ability to set aside difficult problems temporarily, work on something else, and then return later with a fresh perspective.[56]

---

55. Sims, "The Genius of Play," 73.
56. Amabile, "How to Kill Creativity," 79.

Although that part about "plodding through" isn't such great news, it's true also. So, be savvy about how and to what purpose you choose to use your 'incubation' time—it's a coin you'll want to spend wisely.

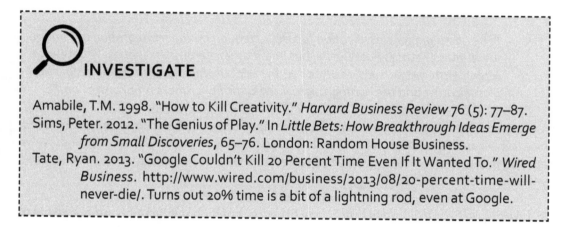

INVESTIGATE

Amabile, T.M. 1998. "How to Kill Creativity." *Harvard Business Review* 76 (5): 77–87.

Sims, Peter. 2012. "The Genius of Play." In *Little Bets: How Breakthrough Ideas Emerge from Small Discoveries*, 65–76. London: Random House Business.

Tate, Ryan. 2013. "Google Couldn't Kill 20 Percent Time Even If It Wanted To." *Wired Business*. http://www.wired.com/business/2013/08/20-percent-time-will-never-die/. Turns out 20% time is a bit of a lightning rod, even at Google.

#29 Converse

> *"The nostalgia for classification focuses attention on the reintegration of romantic inwardness," states Pootwattle; but Smedley vociferously responds, "Pootwattle's intemperate yet persuasive attack on the relationship between the nostalgia for classification and the reintegration of romantic inwardness is unconvincing."*[57]

The author chose to utilize this *prima facie* exemplar of the well-documented, and indeed, nearly inescapable tendency of academic writing to be, well, overstuffed and boring. We've all read it, we've all written it, we've all talked this way, or heard someone who has, and yet despite our shared suffering, it continues.

Put bluntly: no less in libraries than in any other part of higher education, we are prone to lecture. We make long our web pages and wordy our instructive signage. We load students and other innocent bystanders with heavy burdens of instructions and supporting documentation and important tips. We boldly go where no librarian has gone before, seeking to explore the edges of the known universe of how many tabs can be added to our course guides. We are even prone to lecturing when we are, ahem, writing to discourage such behavior. Sorry. Old habits die hard.

What if we conversed instead? What would that look like? Conversations are two-way interactions; they require pauses. They are risky because you are never quite sure what the other person might say, but that is also what makes them interesting and valuable, as we've learned in previous sections (**#16 Listen** and **#17 Translate**).

---

57. Insights by Pootwattle and Smedley courtesy of The University of Chicago Writing Program. 2014. "The Virtual Academic." Accessed March 19. http://writing-program.uchicago.edu/toys/randomsentence/.

Dynamic learning experiences are a dialogue, involving students and instructor, whether that instructor is a librarian, a teaching faculty, a peer or an adjunct instructor. We know this, and there is much evidence that we are putting it into practice across the library community today as liaisons, instructors and collaborators in many roles. Personal connections promote teaching and research; they lay at the heart of an effective library. We are people talking with other people about ideas, helping them think through their ideas, enabling them to investigate still other ideas (as we discussed in **#15 Connect**).

Similarly, dynamic, interesting web content draws you into a dialogue with the author, whether indirect (an internal dialogue you have with yourself and the piece) or direct (a comment, reply, or direct contact). This kind of approach need not preclude us from being substantive, from being 'academic.' Being academic doesn't mean talking like a robot or even always like a peer-reviewed empirical study. To me the question is how best to deliver our top-quality content and expertise in an approachable way, to consciously humanize the tone so that we can **converse** with our patrons and draw them in.

In her article "Content as Conversation", Ginny Redick has four great rules of thumb: space out your ideas with helpful headings; use personal pronouns; stay verb-y; make it easy to scan using fragments and lists. She gives great examples in pairs:

- ☹ The student must register and the fee payment process started before the first day of classes or the student will be purged from classes.
- ☺ You must register and arrange to pay before the first day of classes. If you don't, we will take you off the class list.
- ☹ Upon successful completion of the online renewal transaction, printing your membership card will be an option.
- ☺ Renew online. Then print your membership card.

I like to think of this as writing "business casual." It's still professional, still fit for the office, but it's concise, and not constrained by unnecessary formality. The library web presence must be many things to many people, but it should always be understandable, personable, inviting—human.

INVESTIGATE

Felder, Lynda. 2012. *Writing for the Web: Creating Compelling Web Content Using Words, Pictures, and Sound*. Berkeley, CA: New Riders.

Redish, Ginny. 2012. "Content as Conversation." *UX Magazine*. http://uxmag.com/articles/content-as-conversation.

Sword, Helen. 2012. *Stylish Academic Writing*. Cambridge: Harvard University Press.

Sword, Helen. 2014. "The WritersDiet Test." *The WritersDiet Test*. Accessed March 19. http://www.writersdiet.com.

#30 Leap

I'd like to conclude by talking about endings (which are just beginnings in disguise, by the way). There is a natural human tendency to think that if some is good, more should be better. Sometimes this is true—with ice cream for example. But, even with ice cream (or cake, or whatever your favorite treat might be) you run up against the sad, inevitable truth that too much is ... too much.

This principle applies at every level. It is so tempting to...

- find an overly complex solution to a straightforward problem

I know, instead of a simple list of floors and the call number ranges of books that are shelved there, we could do an interactive map! Using Flash! That we could also write as an app! With crowdsourced metadata!

- attempt to prepare for every possible use case, risk or eventuality

But what if thus-and-so elected official's mother-in-law searches the catalog for a micro-opaque version of a nineteenth-century broadside in Cyrillic script that's located in closed stacks? Shouldn't we first explain the concept of a dark archive before outlining our relevancy ranking algorithm in a splash screen that appears before the search box?

- explain (just to make it clearer) until your users (faculty, staff and students, but possibly also librarians or library staff, or even the public) can't follow (or even remember) the main point (or takeaway) of what you are trying to communicate
- refine and expand something until it's "perfect"

Oftentimes these maneuvers are very well-intentioned, but if you do a bit of digging, they are less about excellence and more about fear. At some point you are going to have to take action. Keep your eyes on the prize: a viable product delivered on time and at (or under!) budget. Avoid scope creep, corner cutting, needless rumination on philosophical underpinnings, frittering.

To create a user experience, there must be something to experience. Starting small is no problem as long as you start; and starting is only meaningful as long as you finish. Sometimes the finish is something you can launch, announce, or open; sometimes it's something you close or correct; and sometimes it's something you decide didn't work the way you wanted so you file it away and move on to the next thing.

Be brave. Try stuff. The more you do it, the easier it gets. Your wings get stronger and you can travel farther. You start to enjoy not quite knowing where you are headed. You might even find yourself someplace you never would've guessed. **Leap**.

Works Referenced Throughout the Text

37signals (Firm). *Getting Real: The Smarter, Faster, Easier Way to Build a Successful Web Application*. [Chicago, IL]: 37signals, 2006.

Allen, Rick. "ROT: The Low-Hanging Fruit of Content Analysis." *MeetContent*, April 13, 2011. http://meetcontent.com/blog/rot-the-low-hanging-fruit-of-content-analysis/.

Amabile, T.M. "How to Kill Creativity." *Harvard Business Review* 76, no. 5 (1998): 77–87.

Association of College & Research Libraries. 2011. "Standards for Libraries in Higher Education". The Association of College and Research Libraries. http://www.ala.org/acrl/standards/standardslibraries.

Association of Research Libraries. 2014. "About | Association of Research Libraries® | ARL®." Accessed June 20. http://www.arl.org/about#.U6SGJqgoxA4.

Basecamp. *Signal Vs. Noise—Business, Design, Programming and the Web*. Accessed April 25, 2014. https://signalvnoise.com/.

Bell, Steven. "The What Versus The Why." *ACRLog*, May 10, 2011. http://acrlog.org/2011/05/10/the-what-versus-the-why/.

Buxton, William. *Sketching User Experience: Getting the Design Right and the Right Design*. San Francisco: Morgan Kaufmann, 2007.

Chicago Public Media. "About Us." *This American Life*, 2014. http://www.thisamericanlife.org/about.

Coleman, Jackie, and John Coleman. "The Upside of Downtime." *HBR Blog Network*, December 6, 2012. http://blogs.hbr.org/cs/2012/12/the_upside_of_downtime.html.

Cooley, Charles Horton. *Human Nature and the Social Order*. C. Scribner's Sons, 1902. https://play.google.com/store/books/details?id=WMA5OJCTCH4C.

Cooper, Alan. *The Inmates Are Running the Asylum*. Indianapolis, IN: Sams, 1999.

Crawford, Amy. "Why the Best Success Stories Often Begin With Failure." *Smithsonian*, February 2013.

Dolan, Gabrielle, and Yamini Naidu. *Hooked: How Leaders Connect, Engage and Inspire with Storytelling*. Richmond, Vic.: Wiley, 2013.

Dudden, Rosalind F. *Using Benchmarking, Needs Assessment, Quality Improvement, Out-*

come Measurement, and Library Standards: A How-to-Do-It Manual with CD-ROM. New York: Neal-Schuman Publishers, 2007.

Edwards, Betty. *The New Drawing on the Right Side of the Brain*. 2nd rev. ed. New York: Jeremy P. Tarcher/Putnam, 1999.

Enis, Matt. "Fail4Lib: Problematic Projects Generate Constructive Conversation." *Library Journal*, March 26, 2013. http://lj.libraryjournal.com/2013/03/technology/fail4lib-problematic-projects-generate-constructive-conversation/.

Follett, Jonathan. "A Practical Guide to Capturing Creativity for UX." *UX Matters*, July 6, 2009. http://www.uxmatters.com/mt/archives/2009/07/a-practical-guide-to-capturing-creativity-for-ux.php.

Fredheim, Helge. "Why User Experience Cannot Be Designed." *Smashing Magazine*, March 15, 2011. http://uxdesign.smashingmagazine.com/2011/03/15/why-user-experience-cannot-be-designed/.

Fried, Jason, and David Heinemeier Hansson. *Rework*. New York: Crown Business, 2010.

Gladwell, Malcolm. *What the Dog Saw and Other Adventures*. 1st ed. New York: Little, Brown and Co, 2009.

Greene, Courtney, Missy Roser, and Elizabeth Ruane. "It's Never Too Late...but Can It Be Too Early?" In *The Anywhere Library: a Primer for the Mobile Web*, 2-8. Chicago: Association of College and Research Libraries, 2010.

Haines, Anne. "New on the Work Blog: All about My #ConfabMN Lightning Talk! #kermitflail https://blogs.libraries.iub.edu/redux/2014/04/30/your-Website-Is-a-Verb-Persuading-Librarians-to-Let-Go/...." Microblog. *@annehaines*, April 30, 2014. https://twitter.com/annehaines/status/461517632102223872.

Halvorson, Kristina, and Melissa Rach. *Content Strategy for the Web*. Berkeley, CA: New Riders, 2012.

Hamilton, Guy. *Live and Let Die* Action, Adventure, Crime, 1973.

Harford, Tim. *Adapt: Why Success Always Starts with Failure*. 1st ed. New York: Farrar, Straus and Giroux, 2011.

Heath, Chip, Heath, Dan. *Made to Stick: Why Some Ideas Take Hold and Others Come Unstuck*. New York: Random House, 2007.

Hess, Whitney. "The User Is Not Like Me." *Pleasure and Pain*, May 4, 2012. http://whitneyhess.com/blog/2012/05/04/the-user-is-not-like-me/.

Indiana University. "Street Smart." Accessed March 14, 2013. http://streetsmart.indiana.edu/.

Jackson, Peter. *The Lord of the Rings: The Fellowship of the Ring* Action, Adventure, Drama, Fantasy, 2001.

Johnson, Steven. *Where Good Ideas Come From: The Natural History of Innovation*. New York: Riverhead Books, 2010.

Kimberly-Clark Worldwide, Inc. "The Kleenex® Brand Story." *Kleenex.com*. Accessed March 14, 2013. http://www.kleenex.com/.

Kissane, Erin. *The elements of content strategy*. New York: A Book Apart, 2011.

Krug, Steve. *Don't Make Me Think!: A Common Sense Approach to Web Usability*. Berkeley, CA: New Riders Pub., 2006.

———. *Rocket Surgery Made Easy: The Do-It-Yourself Guide To Finding And Fixing Usability Problems*. Berkeley, Calif.: New Riders, 2010.

———. "User Profiles." In *Observing the User Experience: A Practitioner's Guide to User Research*, 129–157. San Francisco, CA: Morgan Kaufmann, 2003.

LaGuardia, Cheryl. "My Friend Sarah, the Library Data Analyst." *Not Dead Yet [Library Journal]*, April 15, 2013. http://lj.libraryjournal.com/2013/04/opinion/not-dead-yet/my-friend-sarah-the-library-data-analyst-not-dead-yet/.

Lang, Walter. *Desk Set* Comedy, Romance, 1957.

Lankes, R. David. *The Atlas of New Librarianship*. Cambridge, Mass.; [Chicago]: MIT Press; Association of College & Research Libraries, 2011.

MacEntee, Sean. *Dynamite*, July 20, 2011. http://www.flickr.com/photos/smemon/5977235609/.

Martello, William E. "Serendipity as an Entrepreneurial Tool." In *Academy of Management Best Papers Proceedings*, 80–84. Academy of Management, 1992.

Mediratta, Bharat. "The Google Way: Give Engineers Room." *The New York Times*, October 21, 2007, sec. Business.

Moszkowski, Alexander. *Conversations with Einstein*. New York: Horizon Press, 1971.

O'Conner, Rob. "Personas: The Foundation of a Great User Experience." *UX Magazine*, March 25, 2011. http://uxmag.com/articles/personas-the-foundation-of-a-great-user-experience.

Ono, Yoko. "Try to Say Nothing Negative About Anybody for Three Days, for Forty-five Days, for Three Months. See What Happens to Your Life." Microblog. *@yokoono*, July 22, 2011. https://twitter.com/yokoono/status/94459331394797569.

Porter, Joshua, and Joshua Brewer. "You Are Not Your User." *52 Weeks of UX*, February 12, 2010. http://52weeksofux.com/post/385981879/you-are-not-your-user.

Proust, Marcel. "The Real Voyage of Discovery... at BrainyQuote." Accessed March 14, 2013. http://www.brainyquote.com/quotes/quotes/m/marcelprou107111.html.

Ries, Eric. "Minimum Viable Product: a Guide." *Startup Lessons Learned*, August 3, 2009. http://www.startuplessonslearned.com/2009/08/minimum-viable-product-guide.html.

———. *The Lean Startup: How Today's Entrepreneurs Use Continuous Innovation to Create Radically Successful Businesses*. New York: Crown Business, 2011.

Royse, David D. *Needs Assessment*. New York: Oxford University Press, 2009.

Rubin, Jeffrey. *Handbook of Usability Testing How to Plan, Design, and Conduct Effective Tests*. Indianapolis, IN: Wiley Pub., 2008. http://www.books24x7.com/marc.asp?bookid=25203.

Salkind, Neil J. *Statistics for People Who (Think They) Hate Statistics*. 3rd ed. Los Angeles: Sage Publications, 2008.

Schein, Edgar H. *Humble Inquiry: The Gentle Art of Asking Instead of Telling*. First edition. BK Business Book. San Francisco: Berrett-Koehler Publishers, Inc, 2013.

———. "What Makes Us Happy?" *Atlantic Monthly* 303, no. 5 (June 2009): 36–53.

Sims, Peter. "The Genius of Play." In *Little Bets: How Breakthrough Ideas Emerge from Small Discoveries*, 65–76. London: Random House Business, 2012.

Sinek, Simon. *Simon Sinek: How Great Leaders Inspire Action*. TED video, 2009. http://www.ted.com/talks/simon_sinek_how_great_leaders_inspire_action.html.

———. *Start With Why: How Great Leaders Inspire Everyone to Take Action*. New York: Portfolio, 2009.

Spector, Robert. *The Nordstrom Way to Customer Service Excellence: a Handbook for Implementing Great Service in Your Organization*. Hoboken, N.J: John Wiley & Sons, 2005.

Spool, Jared. "Actually, You Might Be Your User." *User Interface Engineering*, July 22, 2010. http://www.uie.com/articles/self_design/.

Standards for Libraries in Higher Education. Association of College & Research Libraries, 2011; http://www.ala.org/acrl/standards/standardslibraries. Accessed June 19, 2014.

Taylor, Robert Saxton. "Question-negotiation and Information Seeking in Libraries." *College & Research Libraries* 29 (March 2, 1968): 178–194.

Tempelman-Kluit, Nadaleen, and Alexa Pearce. "Persona Most Grata: Invoking the User From Data to Design." presented at the LITA National Forum, Columbus, OH, October 8, 2012. http://www.slideshare.net/nadaleen/persona-most-grata-invoking-the-user-from-data-to-design-14605604.

The Lean Startup. "Methodology." *The Lean Startup*. Accessed April 18, 2014. http://the-leanstartup.com/principles.

Thoreau, Henry David. *The Writings of Henry David Thoreau: Journal*. Edited by Bradford Torrey. Vol. IV: May 1, 1852—February 27, 1853. Houghton, Mifflin and Company, 1906. https://play.google.com/store/books/details?id=8vMRAAAAYAAJ.

Tiger Girl. *Yin & Yang* Photograph, December 29, 2007. http://www.flickr.com/photos/tigergirl/2150432837/.

Turner, Anne M. "Dealing with Angry People." In *It Comes with the Territory: Handling Problem Situations in Libraries*, 45–54. Jefferson, N.C: McFarland, 1993.

Wachowski, Andy, and Lana Wachowski. *The Matrix* Action, Adventure, Sci-Fi, 1999.

WebJunction. "Needs Assessment," April 12, 2012. http://www.webjunction.org/explore-topics/needs-assessment.html.

Weinzweig, Ari, and Zingermans (Restaurant). *Zingerman's Guide to Giving Great Service*. 1st hardcover ed. New York, NY: Hyperion, 2004.

Widrich, Leo. "The Science of Storytelling: Why Telling a Story Is the Most Powerful Way to Activate Our Brains." *Lifehacker*, December 5, 2012. http://lifehacker.com/5965703/the-science-of-storytelling-why-telling-a-story-is-the-most-powerful-way-to-activate-our-brains.

Witkin, Belle Ruth. *Planning and Conducting Needs Assessments: A Practical Guide*. Thousand Oaks CA: Sage Publications, 1995.

Yahoo! Answers. "Where Does This Quote Come From?" Accessed March 14, 2013. http://answers.yahoo.com/question/index?qid=20110506082219AAD4Ckk.

"Kleenex." *Wikipedia, the Free Encyclopedia*, March 13, 2013. http://en.wikipedia.org/w/

index.php?title=Kleenex&oldid=543925345.

Ron Gutman: The Hidden Power of Smiling. TED video, 2011. http://www.ted.com/talks/ron_gutman_the_hidden_power_of_smiling.html.

Sesame Street—"One of These Things..." (Bird Seed), 2007. http://www.youtube.com/watch?v=ueZ6tvqhk8U&feature=youtube_gdata_player.

Author's Notes

This book would have been impossible without the encouragement and support provided by a number of people. I'd first like to thank Kathryn Deiss for suggesting that I write it, for believing I had something to say, for her subsequent patience with my many timeline extensions, and for having been a mentor, inspiration and friend from the very beginning of my professional career.

My thanks to all my colleagues but especially to Diane Dallis, Anne Haines, Mary Popp and Rachael Cohen for their support and flexibility throughout the process. Especial thanks to Diane for supporting my application for research leave at the beginning of this project.

I am grateful for the community of librarians and web professionals whose insights and accomplishments challenge, inform, improve and extend my thinking every single day—there are surely too many to name here, but a special mention is owed to Missy Roser and Beth Ruane: we've been in cahoots a long time and I am the better for it. This manuscript is surely better for your careful reading. To my colleagues on the WeaveUX Editorial Board, a relatively new addition to my professional circle: if only a handful of meetings has yielded so much inspiration and so many on-the-fly memes, I boggle to think what the future holds. (To the rest of you, check out weaveux.org)

I love having written, but not so much always being in that first phase ('to write')—so my thanks and love go out to my parents who have put up with me on the mountaintops ("I had a writing breakthrough today!") and in the valleys ("I hate this book. In fact, I hate everything."). Mom and Dad, you are the best.

Last but not least—Robert, my sweet husband, you and our whirlwind engagement are the best possible reason for pushing my publishing deadline forward (even though really if I'd not have procrastinated on my original plan I'd have been finished before, oh well). Thank you for listening, for talking, and for your constancy and love. You make being married a great user experience.

About the Author

Courtney Greene McDonald is Head of the Discovery & Research Services department at the Indiana University Bloomington Libraries. She has presented and written on a variety of topics, most recently on discovery tools and user experience and on mobile services for libraries, including co-authoring a book, *The Anywhere Library: A Primer for the Mobile Web*. She earned her Master of Library Science degree, as well as a BA in English and Journalism, from Indiana University-Bloomington, and holds a Master of Science in Human-Computer Interaction from DePaul University in Chicago.